BACKLASH
PRESS

A pioneering publishing house dedicated to creating intelligent, vivid books. Established to inform, educate, entertain and provoke.

A Backlash Press Book

First edition 2024

backlashpress.com

Poetry, essay, and photography by Gret Heffernan

ISBN: 978-1-0686972-8-9

Nobody, Nowhere, USA

A lyric essay with photography

Backlash Poetry

American Dangerous: Renée Olander
Bombing the Thinker: Darren C. Demaree
Burial Machine: Jacob Griffin Hall
Clay Unbreakables: Natalia I Andrievskikh
Into The The: Robin Reagler
Phantom Laundry: Michael Tyrell
Tattered Scrolls and Postulates: Joseph V. Milford
The Arsonist's Letters: Michael Tyrell
Unfinished Murder Ballads: Darren C. Demaree
Some Things that have Happened so Far: Gareth Culshaw
Topography of a Woman: Gret Heffernan
Unsent Letters: Gret Heffernan

Backlash Journals

One, Two, Three, Four, Five, Isolation

Backlash Fiction and Nonfiction

The Sculptor: Gret Heffernan
Dark Ansley 01, 02: Gret Heffernan
Life in the Sky Falls Down: Bruce Bromley
The Sky Within: Rebecca Stonehill

Backlash publishes multiple zines, pamphlets, and printed material.

For my mother

Author's Note

I write this because I believe that creativity is the lifeblood of social change.

This is not an account of history; it is a story, which makes it more genuine. Yes, there are facts, and all of them, even the shocking ones, are actual. However, recounting the actuality of an event seldom holds its human truth because time is overlaid and spoken into history. Time is more narrative than fact. In a few incidents, I've allowed myself the liberty of bending time to prioritize emotional continuity over place chronology, but also, because that is how history works. We catch and organize the things that fly out at us. It is human nature to declare what is in our hands as truth. The memory lives as a composite of windfall. And the imagination rebuilds from this debris a structure. This is my structure. And it will affect everyone I have ever loved or sought love from. In order to write it I had to stop longing for their affection.

The cost of this book, for there is always a cost, is the possibility of blood family.

It is the pathways we traverse that imprint us,
recorded by the stories we tell,
they chart our progress and unfold to us our histories,

like the revealing of a map
where the mind and the body
engrave a single terrain.

Redneck

After a lifetime away, I return to the home of my childhood.
I fly from London to Iowa and drive into a hesitation of place
that absorbs me.

The night road, a between phase of selves,
gathers its catchall of memory and parts of our conversations
move through me in small, premonitory gusts.

The pulsation of roadside reflectors. Movement in the ditch. Years.
My mother is dying. We can never see ourselves all at once.

If she dies, I am nothing, I am free, I am fractured, loose cells like idioms
ringing though the history I've surrendered. So,

if our histories become the balance of our misunderstandings,
then art, surely, is the record of our damage and love. You have to decide

the consciousness that you will use to receive this world
and release the grip of what is left.

For me,
that meant everything.

I was born a creationist, a redneck, and all that I knew to be true was orated
inside a chronicle of prejudice, faith, and loyalty.
How long it took to see that

a single word, holds inside it, an infinite number of realms
it employs to define itself, and the place of your birth determines
the measure of meaning you'll inherit.

How alteration comes from redefining the meaning of a narrative
you've known all along.

And, because we carry the language we learn as children,
all my words here are the same.

And, because I've chosen to learn another realization,
all their meanings are different.

How to rectify that? How to communicate without falling
into the known plots of an old skin. There is shame

in my childish desire for affection from those I no longer regard.
And I sense that hidden inside my acknowledgement of their rejection

await promises that I won't be aware of having made
until I'm faced with breaking them open.

There is a grief that accompanies a path unchosen,
however necessary the break may be, it is first the willingness to break
that changes you.

That the crack matters infinitely more than the fallen piece.
and perhaps, perhaps, my only truth is

if I want to speak of the different meanings of words

(which contain whole worlds)

I cannot need to be loved.

The way we position our bodies is conditional to the work we do
and we wear the record of ourselves. And, so –

It comes from working too long in the sun, looking down, head bowed
towards the soil. My families are fieldworkers. It is not red forehead,
after all.

The best part about walking beans is riding through the dawn
in the back of a pickup truck, blowing into a pair of gloves,
listening to the wind and an Igloo cooler full of drinks settling in the ice.
Sky black blue and known bruises on the mind.

The houses mist, blurred from their tattiness and lit from within, beacons
of the rising world across the sparse prairie. It is a void that feels alive.

As though it had once been filled in, then eaten away,
how a brain lost to its memory will keep the body breathing,

the organs laboring – these nameless utilities are ideas we can't catch, on
the edge of worlds far from here, whose doubt we feel, like a little death,

buried and decomposing with the heat of our desire
to be right, to justify the life we have been given.

Nobody speaks. We drive through the rot of ourselves and it is not
unpleasant because it's known, secret in the way that we understand,

having discovered how to endure it. In the middle of the field the farmer
stops his truck and we jump from cab to ground. The road still whistling in

our ears and the soybeans spread as far as the horizon on all sides. Waist
high and wet with dew. We each choose a row, begin to traverse its soggy,

buggy furrow. We cut out the weeds with a hook, pull and stuff them into a
bag. By noon, it will reach around 90°F and we'll have walked beans for

seven hours. Our torsos and heads will be burnt, our feet blistered prunes.
Our legs scratched and cut. Hands numb. Skin bug bitten. Pores pierced by

plant hairs. Cockleburs. And we'll walk through the heat haze towards the
shadow of a tree and sit in its shade. Drenched with sweat and dirty, we'll

eat, drink, and scratch the raw bites on one another's backs. Press Xs into
them with our fingernails. Gossip. Crack our necks, knuckles. But for now,

it is enough to be silent in the cool hours, to find a rhythm to our thoughts that will soon bring the chatter and stories of our togetherness.

Because there is a trust in things unsaid, left to their own devices, inferred through the action of silence. A nod. A handshake. An understanding of what we face. The doubt burning off its glaze of condensation returns to the province of the Others. Here, in this place

that is forgotten, heavenly stars polish the infinite spaces above us and we promise our necks to the sun. A dare that comes from staring at the earth

and feeling the day move over your body as you cut one living thing down so that another can thrive and knowing which one you resemble –

the cut, not the thriving.

There is a kind of hopeful denial born from breathing the seasons, the open sky, and the varied rains, the moral of how long growth can take and then

how sudden.

The Archeologist

My parents met in the Sonoran desert. My mother had become a
hippie to escape Christian Fundamentalism and my father had just
returned from Vietnam. Sometimes you need to step out of your life
in order to retrieve it. The fury when salvaging is intense and I was
soon born in a trailer not far from the border.

We often drove our old jeep into Mexico and dug for bones. At the
time, Mexico was safe, though lawless, and we could dig wherever we
wanted. My father longed to be an archeologist. But the war had left
him an alcoholic. He'd map an area to excavate with beer cans full of
sand while my mother set up camp.

In the evening, a cerise the color of poured pomegranate darkened
the sand dunes into a silent council. And my father would sit inside
the circle he'd made of his artifacts – iguana bones, sockets, car parts,
boat parts, broken pottery. Mother twisted dough around a stick and
held it in the fire. She'd unravel my hot bread and watch a dome of
stars absorb the faint lights of the distant village. Beyond that spread
the sea of Cortez and the giant squids that shipwrecked my dreams.
As soon as the stars were entirely unlimited, my father would
stumble into the village and take Viola, his favorite whore.

When my mother finally left him, she told me, "He did not fight for you," as she put me in the Buick alongside our suitcases, her golden hair aglow, "he asked only for the television and the dog." Then, she never spoke of him again.

He sent three postcards in 17 years: (1) a picture of his campus that told me he had graduated with a degree in archeology, (2) a picture of the Amazon River that told me he'd married the woman of his dreams, and (3) a picture of the Loire Valley that told me I had three sisters. I would not save these cards from a fire, though they consume as much of me as anything I'd retrieve from flames.

My mother carried her depression in and out of jobs and welfare states. She'd listen to Joan Baez and smoke in the dark, staring down at another windswept car park. "You need a winter coat," she said, and, finally, rang her family. She explained that she'd left an abusive alcoholic, but they didn't listen, divorce is a sin, she was told, and we all have our crosses to bear. Her cross was one of shame and ridicule. To carry the weight of it, she filled herself with all the wrong things.

We moved to a rural tundra. Everyone we knew believed in creationism. A woman carved from the rib cage of man left us with very little breathing space. Eventually, her cross became a cancer and they punished her even when she was suffering. All of the worst people I know are Evangelists.

The trick is to find what rescues you before you slip into violent avoidance. You escaped, Father, because you loved something that required learning. That was your gift, despite the truth that in order to receive it, you had to escape me. I am a parent now. I know children develop inside the measure of a parent's compassion. How little you must have loved. And, I see you now, in your respected role, where you seem as ridiculous as a miracle is a lie. This, too, a lesson.

We create for an imaginary other, transfer and counter-transfer, fracturing to build something as complete as it is endless. So.

When I say that you haunt me, I mean that you make me feel unfinished, still forming, and returned to like a compulsive idea. But ideas are grounds to construct upon and you are a current of absence, swirling, encircling our history. To pin a thought upon you I have to develop a memory for us.

I have to improvise a dialogue that coaxes the child you abandoned to come out. Into the firelight. Fulfillment, I tell her, has nothing to do with conclusion. It has to do with cannibalism. Knowing the parts of yourself to eat. Childhood. Fantasy storylines. The time that happens to you. Think of these things as meat.

Tenderness

I arrive at the Holiday Inn and park my rental car. It's early morning and I stand outside the lobby door finishing a QT coffee that tastes similar to how I imagine ground basalt and rat might taste.

The concierge waits, watching me."Bad luck," he says, "that's the worst coffee in the whole state."

"Well, at least things can only get better." He asks me a question I get asked daily when visiting America, "say, where you from?" My accent has taken on a British lilt. "Here, but I've lived in England for twenty years."

He asks if there is any chance I might know his cousin so 'n' so in Manchester? No, I don't. He supports Man U and comically hexes me when I tell him I'm a West Ham follower. He was born in Rwanda. He and his grandmother escaped to Kenya during the Hutu Genocide in 1994. The year I graduated high school. Then, he moved over here when he was twenty-two after finishing a degree in hospitality. He waited until his grandmother died peacefully of old age, "like everybody deserves to do," he said and crossed himself.

To put himself through night school in Nairobi, he worked in the flower fields, "did you know that most of the world's flowers come from Kenya?" And what he'd really like to do is study botany, which he didn't realize was an actual science until he'd moved to America. He thought the science of growing things was in their story. He heard all the stories of flowers from his grandmother. He thinks she told him those stories so they both could manage their losses. All of his grandmother's children, including his mother, were killed by the Hutu.

"Tell me the truth, can you really stay happy living with so much rain?"
"No, but that's what tea, lager, and vitamin D supplements are for."
We laugh and I'm aware of how relieved I am that our conversation is light and Western again.

"Okay, that's some good advice. You see, I got a friend in Seattle, and he says to me, you come on out here, and I'll give you a job in the garden center, that's why I asked you about the rain, besides that, the weather is not too hot and not too cold, and my friend tells me that folks out there, they follow the weather. You see, the key to happiness is the key to growing things, and I've grown plants enough for the garden of Eden, but the key to it all is, you just gotta keep what's tender outta the extremes."

A man arrives and asks him for directions to Bruggers Bagels. He excuses himself, takes out a town map from his back pocket, and spreads it against the window. We say goodbye and I enter the lobby.

A group of young women, blond and groomed, are on a spa weekend. *Oh. My. God.* Between smacks of chewing gum, they compare treatments available. *I am so getting that.*

A bus of Little League players arrive with their families. Everyone is in khaki shorts. They want to know if there is time for a swim in the pool before breakfast at Johnny's Grill and will there be waffles.

Ten minutes later, inside is the cold efficacy of anywhere America, I sit down in the middle of my hotel room floor. The womb of the intermediary. The whirr of silence. The water pipes. A family in the next room turns on the news. I make a pot of coffee and ring the hospital. *She's sleeping and can't have visitors.* I ring room service and order eggs and hash. Eat in the dark.

Later, I walk downstairs to have a look around. I feel nostalgia for a comfort and ease I have never known in this country. I wonder how we can live side by side and have such different experiences of the present. It is clear that my time spent living here was vastly different from the lives lived by those in the lobby. It's hard not to feel a little resentful at the family relaxing on the leather sofas, reading magazines. The grandma with her skinny, tanned legs in golf shorts and Keds. The father with a crew cut and a blue polo, the mother in a tee shirt with a sequined American flag rifling through a Coach bag.

Both my husband and I have worked hard to climb from working class to middle class because we thought it would be better. And it is. A million times better. Anybody that tells you different has never qualified for food stamps. But it comes at a huge cost. That cost is belonging. That cost is knowing how great an injustice it is to the planet and her people that a Western commitment to delusion is required for my everyday life to continue. I do what I can, but I'm fully aware that it is not near enough.

I don't know how to remedy my awareness of our inequality, I feel too much is at stake if I opt out of conventional living. I can only talk about it with honesty. In my experience, those who have opted out are almost always funded by the extreme end of capitalism. They have the cushion of inheritance and the privilege of education and class opportunities. They don't have to worry about ailing parents or their children's education or a mortgage. The year my mother was diagnosed with cancer she was given the pink slip and told that she needed to move house. She was fired upon her diagnosis. She had never owned a property before. We spent our pension buying her house, then we remortgaged our own house to help pay for her radiotherapy. Let me summarize the vice hold of unchecked capitalism. When I found out that she was hospitalized I thought two things in one breath: How will I cope if she dies? How will I pay for it if she lives?

The week before my mother collapsed, I'd heard a story about a woman who had been found in an apartment in London. She'd been dead for two years. Nobody reported her missing. She was twenty-five. The television was still on. For days, I could only think of the TV dramas, the news reports, the commercials that flashed through the room while her body disintegrated. It seemed a tragic analogy of humanity's genocidal loneliness. Nobody, nobody missed her. How does that happen?

When my mother missed a second day of work, her boss, a young, kind woman, sensed that something was wrong. "It was uncharacteristic," she said, and, trusting her gut, drove to my mother's house, thirty miles away, and knocked on her door. The cat was meowing. The television was on. My mother's car was in the drive, but nobody answered, so her boss went around banging on windows and shouting her name until she saw her slippered feet splayed on the floor.

The paramedics broke the door down. Septicemia had taken hold of all of her organs. I went to high school with the man who saved her. "She had fifteen, maybe twenty minutes left," he said. "But I ain't the one that saved her. Her boss did that. She's one lucky lady."

The truth of anything waits for you to find it on your own. Reaching it alone is often the condition of discovery and it doesn't often appear as a story that's familiar. I kept asking myself, would I have done that? Would I have trusted my instinct enough to drive thirty miles and knock on an acquaintance's door, let alone bang on the windows? No. I would have told myself to mind my own business and made excuses. Even though I consider myself an intuitive, loving person, which made me think about the truths I wanted to act upon, not just blithely accept them as inherited character. Because to act is to claim responsibility.

How easy it is to spend our whole lives inside stories that don't represent the truths of our actions, or even the character that we identify as ourselves, when the narrators are those we want to love us, those we feel should love us, or even, our own deceived selves.

Before I left London, I rang my mother's sister to tell her that she was in hospital. I needed to find out what to do if she was released. Her sister has a care home facility and knows about septicemia and rehabilitation.

"Listen, your mother's body is shutting down. You just need to get over here and find a place for her to go after the hospital releases her. I'll have my son ring the hospital and find out their protocol but, honestly, we just can't have her here. It's too much. I have to go. I need to take my grandkids swimming." It was the last time we spoke.

She sent flowers. "Praying for you, God bless," read the card.

I didn't bother ringing her brother. They lived a five-minute drive from one another during the time my mother was undergoing chemotherapy and radiotherapy for bowel cancer, and he never once phoned or visited or even acknowledged that he knew that she was ill.

"You still voting for that damn nigger?" he asked, when he saw her at a barbecue six months after her first clear scan. This was just before Obama's second term. "Obama care saved my life, of course I'm voting for him." My mother told me over the phone, "he just huffed like my life wasn't worth saving."

The difference between a Trumpster and a fieldworker is as stark as the difference between an Evangelist and a Christian.

My mother is the only Democrat in my family. Her political stance has cost her her kinfolk. In their minds, she altogether died when she started campaigning for Hillary. They love Trump and a Capitalist God. "Trump is a Christian man just like your uncle," my grandma said. "That is absolutely true," I said. "See now," she said, "there's something we agree on." My uncle is an absuive man who inseminates hogs. By hand. All day. Make of that what you will.

"Don't worry so much about it," my mother tells me when I get upset by how they treat her. "Seeking their approval all the time is probably what gave me cancer in the first place. I'm better off putting my energy towards healing my own regrets, not trying to get them to admit and attend to theirs."

I was the only family member who visited my mother in hospital, but she was not alone. Every day, women, friends, colleagues, flooded her room with praise and encouragement and support. In the hallway and out of view, they'd cry and squeeze my hand. We'd walk to the car park together. "If you need anything, anything," they said, "just holler." Then they'd pull away in their Broncos or Rams. Each one of them the wife or the daughter of a laborer, each one a patriotic and God-fearing Christian. Then, I'd sit in the car, listening to the rhythm of the evening cicadas, collecting the threads of myself enough to drive.

I'm regretful to say that I have often thought of my mother as a weak woman because she has not sought an education or investigative pathway, however nontraditional, like I have. But also, I've realized, because focusing on her weaknesses conveniently validated the narrative of what I feel I've risen above, which is a form of mistaken self-importance and exactly like my family. I understand that my family and I are opposites of the same fire, the same injustice, and so carry the same conceit. I have to admit this if my story is to be honest.

What I mean is that it's easy to be a middle-class agnostic in England. It's easy to blame Trumpster Republicans and gullible or exploitative religions. To blame greed and capitalism. It is not easy to see your personal role in the problem. We seldom know the lies we're willing to believe for our own validation until something shifts us into viewing them from a different angle, and we're ready to look outward.

My self-righteousness prevented me from seeing the strength it has taken my mother to become a moral thinker and a Democrat in rural mid-America. She has had to rebuild a family for herself from scratch. She is the one who suffers our blood relatives' exclusion. She's the one who is not invited to barbecues, Thanksgivings, Christmases, gatherings of cousins, birthdays, while I sit in comfortable, liberal England pontificating about the importance of education and a world view. What an asshole I've been.

I have to admit that she finds her strength through her God. Who am I to criticize that? These women, her new family, who arrive with casseroles and kindness, wearing little gold crosses around their necks, who am I to judge them? They are not a part of the capitalist or the intellectual clique; they are the fieldworkers who have financial worries and families they are looking after. If the thing that saves you is moral, why judge it?

I found a care home for her to rehabilitate in. I prepared the house for her, the physiotherapist, took her to doctors' appointments, kept her fifteen different medications organized, helped her on the toilet, everything. During the months it took for her to begin to walk again, I thought, if her siblings ring once, just once to see how she is, how I am, how we coped, offer help or show kindness, I'll never put this in writing.

Those summer evenings, after my mother had gone to sleep, were the first I'd had alone in over a decade, since the birth of my children. I sat in a cooling dusk full of birdsong and thought and wrote what would become the backbone of this book. I believed I was writing a farewell letter to my family, but I wasn't, I was writing a farewell letter to myself. The counterbalance that I had had to become to believe myself passionately credible enough to oppose extremism. I believe in my voice now. I want to give voice to my mother.

In the end, your integrity sits inside your actions. I thought I was being intelligent, but, it turns out, I'd just switched tribes. I'd just adopted the prejudiced views of people I wanted to emulate, so the same pattern applied. It was a way of hiding. I understand that now. I understand that I need to live and share all of who I am and who I have been because you can't meet fury with fury and expect to find reason. You can meet it with grace, with honesty, with empathy, in the middle, where diplomatic philosophies have the greatest chance at developing and real conversations, the only things that will bridge us, can take place. I remind myself, again and again, we only grow by keeping the tender out of the extremes.

Redneck

I am not fully the person you know. Is anybody?
Dormant scenes I'd forgotten as familiar –
Hollyhocks rubbing against the machine shed. Jack-in-the-pulpit.
The dander of mown hay. Red thunderstorms –
all waiting to push through and flower
inside new sediments. Lumps of truth
in my throat.

The truth is like that. Dirty and biased and personally tailored,
which means it's dishonest and irrelevant
beyond its abstract storyline. But, we crave it anyway,
call it universal, when what is actually universal
can only be felt.

The feeling of your absence is my story, my truth, alone.

Still, it is strange that I should think of my father in this land.
Strange because I have no memory of him being here – he has
never come anywhere that I am – but his absence was last felt
acutely here. This is the place
where his silence was at its most active.

And so, his presence lingers in a way that I recognize
as the presence of the dead, which is also the presence of my belief in my
childhood God.

The absent, can narrate our lives in ways far more powerful
than the living because they take residence inside us.

I feel his memory, and although he is not inside it, my old hope
of his arrival, his love, is.

I am struck by how desperately I wanted them both to love me.
To see me as laudable, respectable, worthy. It is why I've been afraid
of exposing myself because it might prevent them
from one day filling the loss,
so devoted I've been to patterns
forged by invisible forces..

It is easy to love folklore.
And that's what you are.
Much harder to love the entirety of the self.
I guess I just wanted to say that

it is over between us. I've begun slaying old idols.
There is no point hiding for the sake of reconciliation.

There is only the lightness that comes from the forgiveness
you offer yourself. The mind yields to a thoughtful life
as a form of testimony.

Of seeing myself through your deficiency
as a form of mythmaking.

A child loves a parent, whatever the shape,
and if that shape is nonexistent, then a child learns
to equate longing with nothingness,

love from nothingness, companionship from the imaginary.

And so, I spend my life creating people.

Father, you were the first.

In Hy-Vee, bagging my lettuce, I see an old schoolmate.
"I heard about your mom," she said. "I'm so sorry. What will you do if, you
know, if she passes, is there anyone to help?"
"No, not really."
"What about your dad?"
"I don't have one."
If my mother dies
I will be an orphan.

The need to feel connected to history makes me leave the house in the
predawn and drive to the Effigy Mounds National Monument.

Where I walk and imagine how prehistoric Native Americans shaped
the artifacts of their lives, the things they loved or thought were useful,
into meaningful prayers that could only be seen by elevation. Marching
Bears. Hawks. The contours of grand-scale poetry.

And it feels like a place of ancestral transition, where the woodlands
end, the prairies begin, and the Mississippi continues in a manner
that makes you think of each life as a single molecule of water in
perpetuity of river song. Until we no longer matter. You.

Great Bear Mound is forty-two meters long.
I sit near a paw and eat an egg and cress sandwich.
The trauma of patriarchy has stolen many properties from our bodies –
land, water, flesh, childhood – soiled and lost. To think, now, to feel

as a human connected to the living world involves an
inescapable sense of disgraceful trespass that is only erased through
evasion and the rewriting of reason.

Similar, I suspect,
to how my father feels about me.

Often, I think about the correlation between an absentee father,
any father, it doesn't have to be mine,
and the lack of companionship, guardianship over this planet.

What does it mean narratively
to be fatherless and American?

What does this mean in a culture that narrates its trespasses as the
consequence of progress? To be part of a lineage, a parent, that narrates
their trespasses as consequence of progress?

What happens when the story you've learned
about yourself is shameful?
And what to say to my mother now?
We believe in different ideologies, yet –
I want my words to lead me to my emotional reality,
just as precisely as our silences have done.

Because words are social incidents that proclaim
the vows we've made to living.

I need to be mindful of all that I keep alive.
In me.

Because what I've kept alive
has wrought harm
to myself, the earth, and my fellow humans.

Perhaps this is true for most redneck creationists or any other group
whose actions are not entirely compatible with the words they identify
as their social truths. *We're praying for you. God bless.*

What does that mean for our collective emotional integrity?

Words are the fabric you don your trials inside,
actions give them life. The problem is
that it's become normal for our words to live far from their realities.

I'm telling you this because I want a meaningful conversation
where we both admit a confidence that's been lost and grieved

for the chance of discovering a new place to search for understanding,
not, and this is important, to forget or trick or convert.

But to build upon the strength of a collective awareness
that is reached when separate experiences decide to fold their words
around and touch the vows they've made to the living, breathing
unanimity.

Wrongs have been done, and they need to be articulated because we
are our histories, and we carry these injuries at a cellular level.

This conversation attempts to erase the faces of those
I've been waiting on to interpret my authentication.
My father, but also, all fathers.

I mean to melt my experience
into the formless dimension of sentience
and be enough, by myself, fatherless, motherless, bodiless, for all.

It takes a long time to learn that contentment does not mean a sense
of totality, rather a sense of actively linking parts of ourselves into

that which ceaselessly fights to grow. The planet, the counter-wave of tolerance, science, love.

The very narration of ourselves as a living, breathing language. Where we choose to shape the landscapes of the words

we leave behind with care,
offering instructions for propagation
over phantoms.

It is possible to belong to a place and not belong to its definition.

My hometown in the vast and nameless, provincial, invisible, middle. Where deer drip from slit throats in garages and shotguns are christening gifts. Pink for a girl, blue for a boy, Christian names engraved on the barrel. My cousins and I used to climb up hay bales with loaded rifles and small children on our backs. Grasshoppers scraping our legs and heat rising from the hay like steam as we'd shoot out the windows in the old house.

Every farm had a homestead, left to rot along the wagon trail. Haunted, often burnt to the ground, but nature's markers remained: wild rhubarb

growing in patches, berries, oxeyes, onions, graves. Always large and small. Always juniper trees to keep the soil binding, bound, like our unrelenting respect towards the dead. Birds lived in the houses, sometimes hobos, and, later, meth whores. Before we'd shoot, we'd elect someone to search the inside for potential targets, remembering the eaves with hornet nests. We'd sift all kinds of things: bottle tops and beer cans, panties, old insulating newspapers, burnt spoons. A bible covered in a pile of bird droppings that looked like a burnt-down candle.

There were legends about lights flickering on the prairie and women searching for lost children or husbands, which we took as souls. There were the stories about certain barns where entire families had been found shot, burnt, butchered, or hung, which we took as nightmares. We left those spaces alone because we understood abandoned places, being abandoned ourselves, which was something we didn't talk about, though there were measures of desertion and we all knew them. There were the children that had flooring or incest or alcoholism and the ones that didn't. And that decided your position on the school bus. There were pickup trucks with Igloo coolers full of beer, and dogs, and kids with wild blowing hair. On the weekends, we'd return a cab full of empty Coors cans and, feeling rich, buy everyone Dairy Queen. And field kegs, and water moccasins, and snapping turtles. There were scars from combines, bulls, dogs, and disappointment. There was joy and song had meaning like church or firefly engagements and poison ivy. A missionary or a soldier was a fine job. A teacher was best.

When I moved to the city, I was struck by the inability to verbalize my past when it remained so invisible inside my surroundings. How could we be of the same country? It was like explaining a fable as true. Unreal like living underwater is unreal, yet can reflect to us our image, albeit surface-based and distorted. My measure of humanity is not in the gloss, but in the spit, the grit. What does it mean to leave? It means living in the backwash. The nowhere. A smear to one side. A traitor to the other. Not the carcass or the warm breath, just the knife that knows how to gut things. Cold steel and alone.

It is not the only field I know. Inside of me, lives another field.
It is my frame.

I seeded it as a child, from the dark interior
of a rented apartment in Wyoming. I sat at the window and placed
myself in the middle of the grassland, inside stirring whitecaps of light
beneath an arch of exhibitionist sky.

Beyond, the Bighorn Mountains gnawed the horizon with their omens,
a foretelling of what I was quick to learn –

that there is no freedom without threat,
no life observed that isn't a casing of the imagined,
that few get the love they deserve. But

there are places that we can enter and draw images of ourselves,
to create, to undo, and recreate the pieces of flesh, real or imaginary,
that we've lost or had stolen.

It is a way to reconfigure our historic bodies,
until we pattern some sort of understanding,
not peace, but the reckoning of its absence.

To create is to be a part of the instrument that accesses new realities.
It takes a violent mercy.

Here, in my field, I am honest. I say what I mean to say.
It is the only rule. And so, I must tell you

how often my field is the windblown hesitation of an eclipse, the colour
of concrete, the sirens of wrong. The pieces of me lay hidden in grass
and my mind is a fly crawling inside my dead mouth.

I was murdered on a gravel road in 1989. You should know this about me.
You should know that of her, I kept little. Damage, hair. Yet,

all that I've misplaced finds it way here. Though, it is impossible to
enter the same field twice, which is true for all bodies, think water,
think human, and reality only needs to show you how you live. How
you continue to live.

It only has to let you live out possibilities.
To search, to recover, to dart in and out of selves.

The field is a place between worlds,
and joins no allegiance with time, so can be reimagined.
I can be reimagined. We. Though not without sacrifice.

Once, while walking along a soybean field
I saw a buzzard drop a small animal from a great height.

As soon as she saw me, she flew to her nest in the pines and watched
as I approached the creature.

I knew it was a mouse from its tail and ears, everything else was crushed
into a sack of brown pelt.

This is how a buzzard softens her prey for her fledglings. From the base
of the pine, I heard the young shrills of hunger, and it occurred to me
that reconciliation without violence is a placating idea for society
when, in reality, there is no escaping the fall.

The tenderizing of debris. As heavy as a country in your hand.
Of humanity,

the only option in falling is deciding how we'll break.

The Whore

They lived in a double-wide trailer near the grain merchant. Two women, possibly sisters, with ten kids between them. Trailer trash, they were called. Cigarette butts in the grass. Babies in saggy diapers and nothing else. *Bringing the town to ill repute.* It was rumored that they were whores, and later, once meth was involved, it was confirmed. *But, what can you do when some folks are just born bad?*

During the pre-meth years, every Christmas Eve, after candlelight Mass, my mother and I would leave a black garbage bag full of presents on their porch. Small things, a teddy bear, a pair of gloves, a bottle of Debbie Gibson perfume, shoes, barrettes, scented pencils collected from Dollar General or the Half-Price Store throughout December. We never told a soul. "It might embarrass them," my mother said, "hard people have nothing but pride for protection." But, really, it was a gift unto us, because it was so rare that we could be generous with something material that it made us giddy with the exceptionalness of it – the opportunity to demonstrate the compassion we hoped to someday find.

It lessened, through balance, the shame of the times we'd had to hide from the landlord, crouching low in our apartment's windowless kitchen, fists clenched. The times when our electricity was turned off or when we couldn't afford the Laundromat. How I'd learned to walk with cramped toes. How we'd learned not to answer the phone

because it was usually a debt collector, so would breathlessly count
each shrill until they stopped at eleven and we could breathe again.
How we couldn't pay for breakfasts at the childminder, so I would sit
and watch the other children eat, until eventually the wife gave me
a bowl of Fruit Loops and the husband threw me out, said his wife
wasn't taking charity cases and that I was nothing but a freeloader.
I sat on the curb all day until my mother came to pick me up. I was
seven years old and we went to the hardware store and cut another
key to the apartment door.

I grew up with the anxious nausea of social stigma. The look in a
parent's eye when their child asked if they could have a play date
with me is a look I've spent my life trying to erase from the mirror.
But on Christmas Eve, we got to feel greater than the sum of our
circumstance, noble even, and it carried us through because we'd set
something golden in motion, however small, however naive, we felt
there was a wave of luck that waited for us.

We sat in the darkness of the car, cold clouds of breath, until the
bag was noticed and shadows around the Christmas tree lights let us
know the presents were being put in place. Driving home, I looked at
my eyes reflected on the dark window, the frost and the stars, and I'd
pray that I'd escape and become someone worthy with the means to
be helpful.

When the trailer became a meth house most of the children were
taken into foster care in Des Moines. One sister disappeared, I don't
know where she went, maybe she died, and the other went into rehab
in order to keep the remaining children. After this, my mother said,
"There's poor and there's poor and we want nothing to do with that
outfit," so we stopped leaving presents.

Years passed. Rehab didn't work, but the children were considered
old enough to basically look after themselves. The eldest daughter
was called Wendy and she was a year younger than I was in high

school. Our guidance counselor, a smart, tireless woman called Mrs. Johnston, set up a mentoring program and asked me to meet with Wendy once a week. "Just to talk," Mrs. Johnston said, "and see what comes of it. I understand she's having a hard time but she won't open up to me." It was rumored that Wendy was a prostitute for her mother's habit. She was sixteen.

We met in the art room after lunch. She had the meaty smell of dirty clothes mixed with Aqua Net hairspray. She wore frosted pink lip gloss that glued in the corners of her mouth and she needed braces. Her arms had the purple blotchiness of the perpetually cold.

"I'm no slut," she said, as soon as Mrs. Johnston left the room. "I never said you were." She had a Lisa Frank dolphin notebook that she always carried around. On each page she'd drawn a stickman in the corner, a flip book, and when she ran her thumb along the pages he did a jumping jack. She flipped him over and over and we sat watching him jump. "No, but all ya'll think it," she finally said. It was true. "I know, I'm sorry," I said, and took a pen out of my backpack. "Do you want to play tick-tack-toe?" So we played until the bell rang and she walked out. The next week she was late and stank of cigarettes. "It's my only time to smoke," she explained. I opened the window. Pulled out my Camel Lights and handed her one. She smiled, sat on the sill and lit up. "Can I ask you somethin'?" Smoke coming out of her nostrils. I nodded, yes. "Why is your cousin such a bitch?" She inhaled and continued, "I ain't done nothing to her and she wants a fight."

My cousin was a sports star, a bully hyped-up on adrenaline, and my family's, as well as the teachers', darling. I wasn't. I was terrible at sports and that's what mattered in my family. My cousin and I hadn't really spoken in years, but I was the only person that wasn't afraid of her, because we'd loved one another as kids. Blood was blood.

"Meet me by my locker at last bell and I'll drive you home," I said. She looked at me like I was committing social suicide, which I was, but, "Fuck it," I said. "Maybe you was adopted," she offered by way of explanation, laughing, "I think I was. I think my real momma done left me on the porch."

We walked out to my car together. My cousin was standing with a group of friends in the parking lot. She glared at me as I opened the door for Wendy. A boy shouted, "You taking the trash out?" and everyone laughed. I got in the car and flipped him off. "Lame," I mouthed and Wendy grabbed my hand, "Don't!" she said and ducked in her seat. "Why? He deserves it," I said. "I don't know," she looked out the window, humiliated, the cold, gray day and her small shoulders, without a warm coat, chapped hands, girl-like, a kicked dog, and I just knew she was sleeping with him. "Oh my God," I said, "please tell me that what I'm thinking isn't true." She shrugged. "He comes round sometimes," she bit her fingernail. "It's not like I charge him or nothin'."

The next morning, I went in early and spoke to Mrs. Johnston about it. She said she suspected as much and coached me on what to say. Tell Wendy she's paying him with her self-respect. That he is stealing her self-respect. Tell her that she is not her mother. That what we do with our bodies reflects the image we carry of ourselves in our minds and that image should not be written without her approval. Tell her that she is worthy and valuable and deserves love. So I did. She cried huge, empty sobs and Mrs. Johnston, who must have been listening at the door, came in and held her. After that, Wendy promised that she would attend regular counseling sessions with Mrs. Johnston and I promised to give her a ride home every day. After a few lapses, she finally stopped sleeping with the boy. When this happened, rumors went around that she was so loose you could fuck her on her period and not even feel the tampon. When she walked by the boy shouted, "Hey, what's that whistling? You hear whistlin'? Oh that's jus Wendy's big ol' pussy flappin' round, ain't it now Wendy?"

The stark crudeness of his hate was frightening and had a reversal effect. People stopped teasing her because it was silently understood that he was taking it too far, though nobody challenged him. However, his vulgarity was the very thing that shocked Wendy out of her feebleness. "I know how to handle asshole," she said on the drive home from school. "You don't know the half of it, what I've had to cope with, naw, I know asshole better'n anything. He's meanest when he's sayin' he loves me. Who'd a thought I'd have to go through so much shit just ta like myself? Fuckin' worth it. I can't wait to get outta here."

After graduation, Wendy started working at the local casino and put herself through community college. Mrs. Johnston helped her with her applications for funding. Now, she is a social care worker in Omaha and married to a computer programmer with two children. The only time she came back to our hometown was for her mother's funeral, alone. By then, her mother had moved to Des Moines and the younger children had long been in foster care. On the way back to Nebraska, Wendy stopped by my mother's house.

"I was mowing the lawn," my mother said that evening on the phone, "and you know how I hate mowing, so I was real happy to stop and chitchat for a while. I asked her if she wanted some sun tea but she said she couldn't stay long, just said to tell you hi, to tell you what she was doing. You should see her now, honey, she's unrecognizable. She doesn't even sound the same. I told her so. I said, Wendy, you look so classy and pretty and I'm real happy for you, and she just grinned."

I looked up the boy she stopped sleeping with and found him on Facebook. He is an Evangelist and a solid NRA supporter. There is a picture of him in a red "Make America Great Again" hat holding a shotgun and the rack of a dead buck. They both have the same dead eyes. No surprise.

As for my cousin, she went to college on a full sports scholarship. Within the first few years, she lost the scholarship, gained 200 lbs and bore two children to a deadbeat alcoholic. "I heard her rapid weight gain was because her hormones were wacked out on steroids. It's such a shame because she was good enough on her own. It's just is down to what you're told. Heck, I might not be so heavy if someone would have told me that I was good enough on my own. Did you hear about Mrs. Johnston?" No.

"Well. Apparently, she's always been a lesbian. All this time. I mean we all knew she was into women's rights 'n' all but really she just up and left her husband for another woman, said she couldn't hide who she was anymore. Well, fair play. I'm one to believe that all love is God's love, so it makes no difference to me, though you can imagine how everybody was shocked and some people said that she shouldn't be teaching anymore, I mean what on earth does that have to do with teaching, really, in this day and age, it's ridiculous, you just think of all the good she did, like what she did for Wendy, but nobody brought that up, did they? On accounta her mom being a w.h.o.r.e. and all but that boy was an a.hole and I always feel that w.h.o.r.e.s should have more rights than a.holes because being an a.hole is a character choice and nobodies a w.h.o.r.e that wants to be. Anyways, the scandal of it meant she had to leave town all the same, but it's a lesson for everybody, you know, Wendy, your cousin, dead-eye a.hole and Mrs. Johnston becoming what they were inside all along. I guess we just become who we always were in the end."

Receiving an Education

I went to university on a Pell Grant. That type of welfare grant no longer exists in America. I discovered that the world was divided into two primary groups: The families that had worked in fields and the families that had not.

The poems I had read when I went to university were:
The Epic of Gilgamesh, a few of Shakespeare's sonnets, the Brownings, Psalms.

These words were unrecognizable as human in my world, and may as well have been written by a different species.

I knew more ways to remove a leech, than to read a poem. Yet, freshman year, in the evenings, The Norton Anthology of Modern American Poetry left me euphoric. Suddenly, Plath, Glück, Graham, Dickinson, Carson, it was like discovering the world was round. I fell in love with language. I wrote poetry and got accepted into the undergraduate writer's workshop.

Everyone in the class was invited to the poet's birthday party held on the top floor of a restored Victorian house. I walked there. Alone, anxious, needy.

What would I say to people from places with collective pronouns?
New Yorkers, Bostonians, Chicagoans. I tried to keep the
conversations about poetry,

but the gaps in my cultural experience were noticeable. No, I'd never
been there ... no, I'd hadn't read that ... watched that ... known that
... the final wound was when I pronounced the "gh" in Langston
Hughes, whose poems I'd just discovered and related to as being
poems of the field. The labor inside the call to rise, alighted like no
dead white man could, the profundity of our inequality.

Here, I burned with it.

A woman snorted with laughter and said,
"Who's the hick?"

'70s porn, birthday boy's favorite, lit obscenely on the television, sound
off, the beat of indie rock. I stared at the cellulite on the woman's
thrusting ass, at that moment, I could not have hated myself more.

There are cuts that never completely heal
because to keep them from infection they need to be regularly licked.
I know the taste of myself and this is useful, crucial even.

And, knowing this, what I want to tell her now is:

"I am the poor white, fooled and pushed apart ...
(America never was America to me)."

What dream do you speak of? I know no dream. The good ol' days
were only good for a few people, and always at the exclusion of others.

My grandfather was bipolar. He was a cattleman and farmer.
Indentured servant of the state. He dipped his calves in an insecticide

that a pesticide company told him was harmless. It seeped through his gloves and into the cracks of his hard-skinned hands, where it rewired his mind.

He was often institutionalized and died with the nervous system of a bug. My cousin is a crackhead. His father shot his mother and then killed himself. This is what happens in fringe communities. Disenfranchised people, whomever they may be, know horrible deaths.

The pesticide company gave my grandparents $3,000 to keep quiet, knowing they were poor, knowing that would be an offer they couldn't refuse, knowing their product was polluting the people, the land. My uncle carried on dipping his calves that way. When he hunts, and shoots a deer, he removes the heart and takes a bite out of it while it's still warm. He is a barbarian, in part, because he's spent his life working with poisons and feeling cheated. His mind, along with his land, is chemically treated and owned by people who already see him as a fly, a gnat, to kill.

My other grandfather was a crop duster. He used to fly his plane low over the farm while my grandmother hung the washing out. He would give her a little wing wiggle of affection, releasing powdered insecticide. He was told that DDT was safe. By the age of forty my grandmother's entire body was full of tumors that had metastasized from her breasts. She died a painful, avoidable death.
The dream is no more for them than it is for an Hispanic American, an African American, or any other fieldworker. So, what keeps the redneck from uniting with his fieldworking companions?

The difference is that the redneck believes the dream was created especially for him. That the dream itself is Evangelistic, white, and male, and anyone outside of this vision is to blame for him not receiving his share of prosperity. The more he feels he's lost, the more he hates, for acknowledging his loss as his own ruination, resulting from his own decisions and circumstances perpetrated by his own white, male people would mean acknowledging an ignorance as vast as the indignity at having been manipulated, treated a fool.

There are other reasons.

To dismantle a myth is to always be alone in a crowd.
Who wants a hick in the room?
Who has the patience to understand, or even cares to try, what it takes to unlearn all that you knew to be true? To de-radicalize?

If I speak of my origins, the person before me feels admiration or embarrassment, both of those reactions produce a form of shame that, when accepted, keeps us from ever being equal, so we ignore it, or reposition our relationship around their conclusion.

Sometimes, they simply don't believe me. Mostly, I keep quiet.

Either way, I become an exception to the rule, the rule that the dream exists for us, a minority to my white populace, one that escaped, but isn't that a part of the dream? The escape?

It is easier to believe in myth and superstition than it is to escape, to forsake all who have loved you, as though you had died. And I have died to my family, my childhood. In their minds, I burn in their hell.

Far easier to blame, to hate, to believe in the whims of skies. Locusts. The promise of a delivered salvation. A familiarity with soil we walk upon, till, and bury our dead inside. The fact is,

You never leave the field.

BettyJo

In high school, BettyJo kept the palm of her right hand across her
face at all times. Her elbow tucked against the side of her waist and
her forearm rose across her breast like a plank of pale skin. The edge
of her hand pressed under her nose and when she had a cold, her
hand glistened, then crusted.

Over time, it had been explained, her muscles had grown immobile
and permanently held her hand over her mouth, like some fingered,
bloodless malignancy.

As a small child, she been found by the church or the public authorities,
I never knew, contorted inside an old iron oven. Her father kept her
there between bouts of abuse too demonic to speak of, so she covered her
mouth with determination enough to rearrange her skeleton.

She moved through us, already a memory, already a ghost,
unfathomable in our lockered, primary colored halls.

She wore the fashion of a Methodist grandmother, was thin to the point
of fragility, and walked as though she had to stop herself from running.

A tranquilized doe.

Carrie. Nell. A pre-Braille Helen Keller.

The library assistant was appointed to care for BettyJo. She spent years inching her hand away from her mouth, culminating in the triumph of BettyJo's full-faced graduation photo. The uncovered skin was a rash of pimples. Her eyes had lost their jackrabbit look, now black spaces between stars, became the markers of how the unlearning would be as challenging as the learning.

Now, I live in England, and although I haven't thought of BettyJo for years, she's just crossed my mind. In our village, decades of superstition have kept the albino deer safe from hunters. Eyes, the pink found inside seashells and whistling.

A local herd began breeding with ordinary roe, hides absent their otherworldliness transformed to a mutation of brown and white with the same pink eyes. These hybrids are the favored by hunters because they cannot be defined as one breed or the other, so you get the safety of killing the ordinary and the thrill of killing the extraordinary. One crossed my path and I thought of BettyJo. Ageing in some duplex. Daily visits from an occupational therapist meaning no harm, but demystifying her, and in doing so, opening her up to slaughter like any regular beast.

We are mythmakers and in myths there are sacrifices.

When I am home, in Iowa, I see them displayed everywhere: deer heads, bear heads, pheasants on boards, fish on boards, talismanic trophies of place and perceived powers. Across the world: shark fin, gorilla paw, rhino horn, elephant tusk, lion head.

Evidence in the idea that to kill is to own, to halt mortality is the story a gun enables, godlike in its decisiveness and entitlement.

I remember sitting in a trailer drinking lemonade under a buck's head and thinking, what if we had to display all of our killings this way?

What if we had to own, like a hunter owns, the bodies of the lives we've taken? Human hands, human feet, human heads, hearts of developed-world convenience.

The kids run in and out of an open screen door. The mother butters bread for bologna sandwiches. The father in the yard with a hose. *Last year a flood, this year a drought, and grain prices low again. I could just strangle China.*

Somewhere in Washington, this family's ballots are tacked up on a wall, like any fish, borax full of formaldehyde and sawdust, that once swam free. You, who are the sacrificed, hunted, mined, and baited for your labor, trained to forget the murderers whose faces resemble your own. Trained to forget your own.

Redneck

I open the door to my mother's house. The cat swats at my feet as I walk through the wreckage of her depression. She's in the hospital. I've just come from visiting hours. I bought a Cesar salad in the canteen. Sat alone with all the other people sitting alone. There are no real cures for this kind of melancholy. There are only different ways to live with your

selves – prized together in the idea of attained harmony that we carry in our minds like a dream, waking or otherwise, we fracture and gather, fracture, and gather our way

to light.

Living is a technique.
The pieces of story, of flesh, that are intractable, slotted between those we crush to dust. How gutting it is to shatter that part of yourself that wants love. My mother looks like a child in her sleep, like someone just wanting to be kept safe.

I don't know if her family ever valued her. She was the disgrace. She was abused by my father. When she left him, they blamed her for not keeping the sacrosanct of marriage. When I think of her then, she is never filled in, a phantom, easy to threaten, easy to belittle, victimised by the very people

she turned to for support, who looked at her, and hated the reflection of their own small hearts.

My uncle, the unstable abuser. My Aunt, the delusional perfectionist. My grandmother, the disappointed grudge holder. My mother, the weak democrat. Her political stance gave them an excuse to banish her forever, even on her deathbed, but excuses are seldom reasons.

I believe witnessing her devastation brought into question the fabrication, the holes, of their own decisions, holes that her presence made them face. There is no greater mirror to character than how one responds to another's helplessness.

It would be easy to dismiss them as ignorant and mean. It would be easy to dismiss this essay as political. But.

Ignorance, self-imposed or otherwise, is a form of bondage and people tend to live inside the ideas attributed to them, so unpacking the role of ignorance has value. Our social divide, as well as its antidote, is found in places, the people, the ideas that we purposely ignore because they are radically different to our own. I am trying to see the equal purpose of all things as a driving force for change. Compassion, that motion

towards the edge places of self, where we witness how the brain branches in fractal patterns, like salt flats or river deltas or frost, collecting different geographies of the historic mind. Separating heredities through belief, now, not blood. I am tired of the Us and Them.

Must we, once again, witness the extremes of hate? The repetition of history is subject to our response, our inaction, but we don't like to speak of humans, of countries, this way, because western humanity would like to believe it's learned its lesson. Improved itself. And, yet:

is a child born into poverty equal in the minds of the public and the state to a child born into wealth? To a single parent? With a drug addiction?

With mental illness? What about a child born into an impoverished neighbourhood with failing schools, failing communities, bonded ignorance?

Do our classes not wear markers of identification? Our voices? Our faces? Our exposure? Our public and observant sense of place and position?

There are three pillars of class distinction that determine opportunity: cultural, economic, and social.

Education, social advancement, and economic security are forms of Capital. Ignorance, social exclusion, and economic uncertainty are forms of violence. And when acts of passive violence are accepted by your nation as normal, active violence, towards the self or the public, is the way you learn to express your humanity.

Active violence is where intolerant paradigms of rhetoric, of the lack of compassion, of dismissiveness, takes us. When an act of barbarity, of abuse, is insinuated, ignored, or recognized and mentioned with any level of acceptance, it is repeated. And, repeated.

There were many: chiggers, barn dances, barn raisings, Kraft casseroles, meth heads, combine accidents, snapping turtles, pesticides, preachers, meadows, food stamps, stars, guns.

There were few: museums, books, science lessons, astronomers, degrees, gays, career women, atheists, non-white ethnicities, rust-free cars, artists, politicians, rights.

Speciation involves the splitting of a single evolutionary lineage into two or more genetically independent heredities. Speciation occurs when the same species evolves inside different environments with different experiences. It is a flammable metaphor for political and opportunistic extremisms that aim to divide, which is why reaching for human connectivity is an act of radicalism. Finding compassion for those you'd sooner ignore is a form of constructive anarchy.

I sit on the front stoop with a cup of coffee. The cat on my shoulder like a parrot. Having spent the night cleaning, sorting, I'm fatigued to the point of hallucinating fixation. There is something about the car that bothers me. I get up and walk around it. I look underneath it. I touch the tires, the hood, the windows. Wait a minute. Why is it so clean? Where are all the bugs? Seriously. Where are all the squashed bugs?

Hardly any on the bumper, the windscreen. I've been driving back and forth to the hospital for weeks. One morning drive, one evening drive. In my youth, driving during these times of day caused a mini genocide of insects. You had to have water in your windscreen wiper to be able to see properly.

A boy rides by on his bike. "Hey, come over here a sec' and look at this," I say, pointing to the bumper. "See how it's basically clean?" He gives me a look that reminds me I'm a woman with a cat on her shoulder inspecting the clean bumper of a Taurus at 7 a.m. "Yeah?"

"Do kids still have car washes to raise money?"
"Um, yeah."
"Have you been involved in one lately?"
"Yeeeeah."
"Were the cars really buggy?"
He thinks. "Not really."

"Well when I was a kid the cars and trucks, especially the trucks, were literally caked with dead bugs."
"I guess we're just lucky."
And he quickly rides away.

My mother's house has been unoccupied for three months now. My head is an alarm. It dawns on me that I have found no mouse droppings, no crickets, no spiders, no trapped moths. Just flies. Piles and piles of horseflies. The insects of my youth have vanished. I listen; there is no hum in the air, far fewer birds, and in the evening, when I sit out and have a cup of tea, all I can hear are locusts.

The Meth Head

Brandy was my Aunt Becca's sister. Becca was my aunt by marriage. I have one memory of Brandy before her murder. We are in a farmhouse and Brandy was perming my aunt's hair at the kitchen table. Brandy was a novelty because she had married a Saudi Arabian immigrant named Ali, but everyone called him Alex so they wouldn't have to remember where he was from when they weren't looking at him.

Alex had come to America to provide for his family, who remained in the Middle East. He'd become Westernized over the years, worked as a mechanic, married Brandy, and though he still kept in contact with his family, he'd basically left his religion behind. "He's fallen," Brandy explained. She thought it was sexy.

They had a son called Nate, who was three and my cousins and I were deciding who would get to go first on the tire swing. We each put a foot in the middle. "Eeny, meeny, miny mo, catch a nigger by the toe, if he hollers make him pay fifty dollars every day, my momma and your momma were hangin' up clothes, my momma punched your momma right in the nose, what color was the blood r.e.d., and you. are. not. it."

Brandy pointed a pink curler at us and turned to Aunt Becca, "Did you hear what they just said? Tell them what the hell you just said," she instructed us. We looked at her and realized what we'd done wrong. "We're sorry, but we didn't mean our mommas were really punching each other."

"Is that what you think I'm mad about?" She turned to my Aunt Becca and my mother, who both lit cigarettes in preparation for a lecture. The smell of smoke and perm solution dizzied the air. "What is wrong with you two? They don't even know they've done something wrong, the babies. Letting them say those things, 'specially with Nate around," then she turned back to us. "It's TIGER okay? Goddammit, not nigger, don't ever say that word, it's catch a tiger by the toe, remember that."

My uncle walked in and spat his chewing tobacco into an empty Coors can. "Don't you take the Lord's name in vain in my house. I don't know what you're getting so pissed about. Lookit, we got our own little sand nigger right here," he said, and ruffled Nate's hair.

Brandy clenched every muscle in her face and continued to wrap my aunt's hair around a curler while she said, "I will not have you call him that." Calm and measured.

My cousin and I looked at one another, we were no strangers to the belt, and expected my uncle to freak out, but he didn't, "Okay," he nodded, "okay," and left the room. Between the women eyebrows raised in a silent reverence for Brandy that became, between the children, a silent reverence for Nate.

After that, we pushed Nate first on the tire swing. I held him on my hip and wiped his snotty nose with a leaf. We touched his arms and black hair, he was original and foreign before that had become threatening, so we argued over who got to have him as their baby when we played moms and dads. It made my little cousin jealous; usually she was the treasured, adorable one. "He's not that special. He's just a little sandy." And we took to brushing him off, as a part of our parental duties, having decided to both be moms, and pinky promising one another never to throw punches unless we had no other choice or had received a sign from God.

Alex and Brandy lived in Cedar Rapids, Iowa, up north, where it was more liberal because they were near a university full of famous poets. We lived less than an hour from the Missouri border. Shortly after their visit, Alex's brother had arrived from Saudi Arabia and lived with them for a while. He doted on Nate and, although he was there to bring Alex and Nate back to Islam, he took the opportunity to date an American girl, called Nancy, who became friends with Brandy. Alex's mother regularly phoned her sons and spent hours wailing and crying over their heathen disgrace. She blamed Brandy and Nancy for brainwashing her sons, for the damnation of her soul, and the soiling of their bloodline. During that year, one by one, the whole family moved over and this resulted in frequent screaming matches that became more and more violent. Nancy wanted out, but Brandy was married with a child. The two women decided to run away, with Nate, and seek refuge with family in California.

The night before they were meant to leave, Alex shot Brandy in the head while she slept, killing her instantly. Her hands were folded under her pillow and cheek, which, the coroner informed us, meant that she had no idea that she was about to be murdered, so suffered no terror. Then, Alex sat down and wrote a five-page suicide note explaining that he had performed an honor killing and that Nate was to be raised a Saudi Arabian Muslim by his brother. He called upon Fatwa to clean his family of disgrace, and then he put the pen down, picked up the handgun, stuck it in his mouth, and killed himself.

Nancy arrived with a packed car ready to collect Nate and Brandy. When Brandy wouldn't open the door, she used her key to walk inside and found Nate crying beside his mother. "Mommy has make-up on her face," he told Nancy, "and she won't wake up." His little hands were bloody from trying to rouse her. The coroner said that Brandy and Alex had been dead for many hours by the time Nancy had arrived. Nobody knows what time Nate woke up or even what he witnessed exactly, but based on his early conversations with the psychologist, it is believed that he was awake in the apartment for at least an hour with his dead parents. He was nearly four years old.

Nancy took him straight to the authorities and both Nancy and Nate were put in protective custody, where they remained under the supervision of a state psychologist during the court case.

We were all summoned to my grandparents' house. The adults sat around the kitchen table drinking coffee. It was decided that my uncle and Aunt Becca would fight the Saudis for custody. *There was no way they were going to let a bunch of sand niggers take one of our kin.* The sense of validation mixed with horror came across in everybody's voice. *What the hell did Brandy expect,* was the pervading tone, though nobody said those words until much later. Right now, it was Us against Them and Nate was one of Us because we couldn't lose to Them.

The adults of my intermediate family all had to testify to the suitability of my aunt and uncle as parents. They all knew my uncle was a racist. They knew he used to hold his cousins down and pinch them with pliers. They knew he took pleasure in killing animals, but the Saudis were worse, we were told, after all, they were murderers and didn't even believe in God.

The stories that came back from the courtroom were despicable and petrifying. We were told that the women wore long black gowns, as though they were the devil's ghosts, and they slapped Nate across the face when he spoke. We were told that the men in the family were all terrorists, which meant that their God wanted them to murder Christian people. We were told that each brother had framed the knife he'd used for his first kill, blood and all, and hung it on the wall. I have no idea where these stories came from but I remember picturing them as devil worshipers and feeling, for the first time, truly afraid of hell. I spent that year on my knees praying for every Christian soul.

According to my uncle and Aunt Becca, the state psychologist was *a dumb bitch head doctor that didn't know jack shit.* When the judge awarded them custody, my uncle said, "Damn straight, you think an American judge is gonna choose them? Helllll no. We hadta go to all that trouble for that fuckin' shrink's sake." So it was decided that Nate would not see the head doctor long term, after all, "What the hell does a four-year-old remember anyhow?" So, we told him that his parents died in a car accident and were in heaven. My uncle and Aunt Becca gave him a picture of them to keep in his new room.

Later, it didn't occur to anyone that his disconnected fascination with bodies and morbidity, his sensitivity, his inability to focus, his nightmares, his extreme insecurity, and fears of being alone were the results of early childhood trauma PTSD. They just thought they were the behavioral symptoms of his dad's bad blood. My uncle tried to knock it out of him and chased him around the yard with a hammer. When Nate cried or became overly sensitive, he was told to *stop being such a faggot.*

Only my grandpa spoke up and said that it was wrong to treat Nate this way. That there were other ways to make him a man but, unfortunately, his head was full of a pesticide that had rewired his brain as bipolar, so nobody listened to him.

By the time Nate was seventeen he was addicted to meth and had a criminal record. He knew the truth of his parents by now. Secrets like that are hard to keep in a small town. During his senior year, after a bout at getting clean, my grandpa said that he could come to the farm and work after school. My grandpa was happy to make sure that he stayed out of trouble. Nate was tenderhearted and loved animals plus he had an uncanny understanding of machinery, so was perfect on the farm. Later Nate said that those were the best months of his life.

My grandpa had a baby blue pristine 1950 Chevy 3100 half-ton pickup truck that he'd had from new. It was a privilege to ride in the front seat with grandpa around the farm, so much so, that I vowed to name my first daughter Chevrolet, but call her Chevy for short, and paint her nursery baby blue, even though it was a boy's color.

When Nate graduated high school and got a good job changing tires, my grandpa gave him the truck as a gift, so that he could get to work and start a new life. One day, Nate went missing. We never saw the truck again, but the next time we saw him, his teeth were black and his beautiful brown skin was covered in meth sores. My uncle and Aunt Becca stopped talking to him. My grandpa forgave him. He sat on the back porch and had a beer with my mother and I and said, "I could tell when I gave it to him that he felt he didn't deserve it, not any of it, the truck, the kindness, the good job. I should have known that he'd try to prove himself right."

Nate met his first wife in a crack house. She got pregnant and they decided to clean up. They helped each other with withdrawal and remained clean for a number of years. She went to night school and he went back to changing tires. They had another baby. He was a loving father and as proof of this, I was told, "that crackhead cares more about his little girls than your daddy ever cared about you. Not that it takes much, but you know, hell." It seems crazy, but it was one of the first times my family had ever mentioned my father. I could count the things they'd said about him on one hand: (1) his name; (2) he was an abusive drunk; (3) that he constantly had affairs with other women; and (4) he never paid child support or when he did, it was only a small amount. (5) he traded me for the TV and the dog. That's it.

It was my freshman year at university and I had recently read *No Name Woman* by Maxine Hong Kingston. I was thinking about trying to find my father on the drive home for Easter when I had a flat tire. I was near the mechanics where Nate worked. He helped me out and later sat with me and had a beer. I told him the story had made me want to look up my dad. He said that he thought he might have found an uncle working as a mechanic in Cedar Rapids, but he hadn't contacted him. It was complicated because he knew that being accepted by them would mean never being able to return to us. I felt the same, as though discovering who I was was an act of betrayal.

It is important to understand that we loved Uncle, everyone did, even though they knew he was cruel. He was loud and strong and he made us feel inclusive, which felt more vital than being correct or kind. We were a fringe community, we grabbed at basic survival characters, even if that meant bending our idea of compassion, our idea of abuse, so that it silently fell in line with his. Few people ever verbally disagreed with him and this silence made them complicit, which meant that they fell under the dominion of his ring. That mania that you felt near him made you fearful, yet desiring of his protection. And that was an exhilarating thing because the ability to feel powerful was something we'd never felt before.

When I was little and pretending to be asleep on the couch, I overheard my grandmother on the phone say, "I keep praying she'll find somebody, anybody, to marry her," so I knew straight away that she was talking about my mother, the only divorced woman in town, "at least she was born in wedlock, at least she's not a bastard and Uncle has chosen to take her under his wing, so that's a blessing." Up until that point, I had been endured, yes, loved by my mother, but told I was the reason why she wasn't "marriage material," her weak job prospects, why she couldn't go back to school, was broke, fat, etc., she was martyred by her sacrifice and I was conscious of being a burden. I had never, ever, been chosen.

That was the power my uncle had. He made you feel chosen instead of marginalized. He chose Nate, and in doing so, purposely vilified all other choices Nate might make, so that Nate was tied to him. Nate's family was full of murdering terrorists. My father had gone from being an abusive drunk to an arrogant, liberal academic. The extremities didn't matter, what mattered was that they were the Others, and if we began to identify with Them, it would validate the quiet assumption that we'd tried desperately to cover up, by conforming, agreeing, erasing, the assumption that we'd never truly belonged anyway.

Growing up under dogma and then learning to think critically as an adult, requires that you prove the worst that you and your community have always suspected about yourself true – that they were wrong to choose you, that you were always a hell-bound infidel and undeserving. And you sense the relief they feel, the *I shoulda known*, when you slip, when they begin to wash their hands of you and this becomes your understanding of validation, your allowance of love. So. You can stay and say things, silently or vocally, that you don't mean, until you begin to mean them, or you can risk entering Elsewhere. Let me tell you something about Elsewhere:

Elsewhere doesn't like you. Elsewhere doesn't want you. You embarrass them. In Elsewhere, you quickly realize that you are thought of, silently or vocally, as shameful and ignorant to the ways of the world. Which is partially true, but it's not your fault. In Elsewhere, you realize that everything you thought was true, is wrong, that your language is wrong. We are tribal and we wear our tribes like badges. How we think, our patterns of thinking, determine our tribe. A Saudi Arabian could be accepted as kin as long as they submitted to our ways of thinking. Nate was chased around the yard with a hammer because of his thinking, his actions, not only his skin color. To change tribe is to change the very fabric of your mind.

It is easy enough to look and sound like a different tribe, but very difficult to rewire your thinking, you have to commit to this for life. What you don't realize in the beginning, and what privileged tribes don't really understand, but you do because to get to where you are you've had to intimately examine and consider prejudice, is that when you are born into the tribe with the least amount of opportunity, the least amount of education, the least amount of social and cultural experiences, you are generations behind the social and thinking patterns of other tribes and they judge you for it, even when they say they don't, even when they feel they aren't, you feel them watching, politely, for you to prove what they also suspect is true, that you don't belong here, that you were not the born chosen.

You are the exception, as though you were just a flower seed in a weed bed, blown in by the fates. Being called an exception implies that your outcome could have gone no other way, which isn't true. It patronizes and undermines how hard it is to change the patterns of your thoughts, your ideas about the world, how the work never ends, but they don't see this because they were raised thinking the way that you have had to learn how to think, so they take for granted that critical thought is standard thought, but it isn't. Standard thought is tribal. Also, it is easy for them to think of you as an exception because it allows them to dismiss your tribe, to defer the responsibility of generational opportunity and learnt critical thinking patterns back to the tribes with the greatest poverty, the lowest funding for education and the highest rates of suicide, devotional dogma, pesticide pollution, and drug abuse. "See," they say, about the exceptional black person, exceptional redneck, exceptional Mexican, "it can be done if they just put their minds to it."

How is that progressive? It's the same place of prejudice, just eloquently described as tolerance with quotes and diagrams. Tolerance is not accepting the exceptional redneck (enter any marginalized group of people) that thinks like you, it's turning to the one that doesn't and saying, "Help me understand you, help me understand my function in your circumstance, sit with me and let's discuss this," then listening without judgment, without needing to be right or better or anything other than a fellow human.

Nate never grew up. He just got older, but remained a child needing love. Addiction did his thinking for him and within a year after our conversation he was missing again. His wife, who had stayed clean, filed for divorce and put herself through community college. During that same year, Aunt Becca divorced Uncle, so Nate stopped being our family's problem, having never been an actual blood relative. "Good riddance," they said, "embarrassing us after all we've done for him, the ungrateful son of a bitch."

Years passed and my grandpa died. We tracked Nate down through his ex-wife and he came to the funeral in a terrible state. High as a kite. Scratching, skeletal, paranoid, he had open wounds on his face and was missing teeth. He had been homeless, but was currently living with a friend, while Alex's brother was sorting him out with a job as a mechanic in Chicago. When my grandmother died, my other aunt, the good Christian one, did not include Nate as a grandchild in her obituary. She told him about her death after the funeral so that he wouldn't embarrass us, meaning, her. After that, we didn't hear from him for years. Then, a fluke, my mother got a job working with Nate's ex-wife's mother.

Turns out, he did take that job in Chicago. Alex's brothers intervened, sent him to rehab, and he was receiving counseling for his parents' death. He pays child support. He remarried and had another daughter. They live in the south side of Chicago and take it day by day. My mother saw him at his eldest daughter's graduation. She's an exceptionally clever girl and has graduated high school a year early. Although she'd received scholarships to many colleges, she chose one close to her family because her mother and stepfather have adopted ten children and she wants to help raise them. All ten children come from parents with meth addiction.

My mother gave him a hug and said that he was skinny under his jacket but seemed happy enough, had clear skin, and new teeth. Although they all live in the same small town, my mother was the only member of Nate's family to attend his daughter's graduation party. My mother told me how he gave his daughter a hug and said, "I'm so proud of you. I'm sorry I've been such a fuck-up. You deserved better. At least one of us is doing something worthwhile." And she replied, "Dad, it's not your fault. You're here now, you're better now and I love you and that's what matters." He had to leave the barbecue and sit in his car until he stopped crying.

Not long after I read this quote from E.E. Cummings:
We do not believe in ourselves until someone reveals that deep inside us something is valuable, worth listening to, worthy of our trust, sacred to our touch. Once we believe in ourselves we can risk curiosity, wonder, spontaneous delight, or any experience that reveals the human spirit.

And I thought, yes. Yes.

When you are abandoned there are words you long to hear your whole life – "I love you," "It's not your fault," "I'm sorry," "I'm proud of you," "You have value" – and it takes a long time, a lifetime usually, to realize that what you have been searching for, possibly destructively, is a way to say them to yourself and know them as true.

Redneck

Language depends on relationships.
Meaning, the interpretation of a word adapts
through its interactions within a community.

Our realities are not the same.
It is the regularity of spoken interpretation
that decides the eventual definition of a word.

In this way, words live and evolve
and represent different meanings
inside of different communities.

The same applies to the objects
that embody our beliefs because they symbolize our words.

For example: I write this while sitting at my mother's kitchen table.
I can see the garage and her Democrat banner, an object of her belief.

The neighbors are in their yard and the woman weeds her marigolds.
Her children run around shooting one another with startlingly
lifelike machine guns.

Her husband comes out with towels for the swimming pool. He throws them in the back of a truck with a loaded gunrack, a Trump bumper sticker, and a decal of Calvin peeing on (so-called) ISIS. Maskless throughout Covid, he called himself a defender of freedom.

I have been clearing my mother's house.
She has hoarded for twenty years and uses objects to replace the words she feels unable to speak.

When we can't say what we mean, it becomes impossible to live how we intend, so, something of ourselves is lost and when there are no words to recover it,
we look to items instead.

Yesterday, I asked the neighbors about garbage collection guidelines and they asked me about the health of my mother.

I wanted to tell them that while picking through the pieces of her, I'd found piles of little notes, on post-its, wrappers, envelopes, containing replies, she felt she should have given during political disputes with her family, real or imaginary, I'm not sure.

And earlier notes she'd written to defend, it felt, her right to be alive. In one she says, "I can tell you wish I would disappear or had never been born." Hidden inside the shoe cupboard, in the junk drawers, the basement, the holiday decorations box, the remote-control basket, were countless notebooks, slips of paper, of conversations she wished she would have had, small, handwritten attempts at validating opinions that had been dismissed as illogical, unworthy by the people she wanted to appreciate her. To love her. Yet, for the sake of her privacy, but also mine, I spoke to the neighbors with the polite resistance of knowing one another to be using words with different shades of implication. Avoidance language. Safe. Too safe.

The damage of our political correctness and polite contrivances is that bold and aggressive words are now projected as facts because they are rhetorically brave, not because they are legitimately true.

What does it mean when a word like Liberty is understood as something different to each fragment of society, yet the idea that liberty is a concept that requires defending remains unbroken?

The defence becomes the definition, not the reason for its linguistic divide.

And the greater the divide, it seems, the further we stand from the original meaning of the word, choosing, instead, to illustrate ourselves and defend our actions.

Like drawing only the negative space of a scene and expecting to know each image, each place, each person. It just doesn't work. Nevertheless,

I stood behind forty industrial-sized garbage bags that I'd cleared from my mother's tiny house, speaking politely about collection times, using non-object, outline-only words, despite the real picture decaying in the heat between us.

That love, like home, is a place-idea that you try to protect with the desperation of one who keeps running back into the fire long after everything is destroyed.

Because there are rooms we walk into and never leave.

But division presents challenge as a form of acceptance and there is an ease that breathes after the giving way, of realising

that the words that had felt ordinary until you learned to live their opposite, thereby, defaming and expanding the originals,

need to be spoken about again – this time
with your different tongue –

because the point is not to leave the house behind.
The point is to stand in the middle and tear the structure down from
the inside. That is how you find the unity of emotion.

Written in the margin of a yellow legal pad:

"Maybe someday you'll read this
and you'll see me as someone who mattered."

Says every heart
who's ever fought for freedom.

Gun Control

There were four of us. We were seventeen. We were in each other's
pockets and new discoveries close. I was dating Asshole and Red
was dating Maniac. Maniac and Asshole flirted and drank. Red and
I played cards and cooked. He worked steel and raced motorbikes.
I wrote poems and took walks. We ought to be together, I secretly
thought, but was going to university in August. "Why would you
stay in school if you didn't have to?" asked Maniac, who was working
on her GED. Asshole was passed out by then. I was only with him
because his parents were wonderful people and I craved their
attention. I looked at him, a slug on the sofa. "Somebody needs to
improve us," I said. Red smiled in that way that took off my clothes
and skin. Around him I was always just muscles and bone. "It should
be you," he said and I knew what he meant.

At university, Asshole hung around destroying me until I hit him
over the head with a frying pan and knocked him out. I made a pile
of his things on the lawn, dragged him onto the porch, locked the
door, and went to bed relieved. That morning marked the end of our
relationship. I rang Red and explained how I had tipped over the
limit and shamefully, though not regretfully, morphed into Maniac.
He told me how Maniac was setting fires to everything and dropping
toasters in bathtubs. I told him how Asshole was screwing everyone
and shouting my name from balconies. We decided to commiserate

over coffee. He told me that entering his love would be like entering a witness protection program. I could safely invent an entirely new identity. The plan was to keep our love secret until Manic was emotionally stronger. I agreed because I felt sorry for Maniac, but also, because I could see the divide, though I couldn't articulate it. I had gone normal, you see. I was paying rent, studying Chaucer and filing insurance claims at the hospital. Nothing in my refrigerator was out of date or mouldy. I had fresh milk. The taste of something more, and while Red lived poetry, he did not care to know it. Loving him was fulfilling a desire from my past that I knew had little to do with my future.

I stopped by the grocery store on my way home from work. I had seen a spaghetti sauce recipe in one of the hospital waiting room magazines. I was going through a sauce phase. It started with a dream I had that felt more real than any reality I was living. In the dream, I was a professor of poetry and lived in an old Victorian house. The furniture was sparse, antique, and full of ghosts. Plants in clay potts were everywhere and on the walls hung the artwork of my friends. Rugs on the floor and something always bubbling on the stove. I had invented sauce nights, where the people I loved arrived at the door with a bottle and a hug. I provided them with pasta in large white bowls and some combination of homemade sauce. Regular old Bolognese. Purple pesto. Orange, walnut, caper, and Cheddar. Creamy asparagus. Roasted tomato and almond. It seemed extraordinary to want something so simple, yet so foreign to the life I knew, like realizing an exotic bird at your holding disposal. I collected new recipes in a folder. On payday, I bought ingredients and practiced my skills. I was working towards creating my own secret sauce that I could pass down the generations like a relic to the normal life I'd managed to build for myself. It was past midnight when I got to the grocery store, parked, and entered the humid evening. I remember how the florescent light zombified everyone, how my skin prickled in the air conditioning, giving my quest more gravitas because it felt gruelling, like the end of the world. I remember sniffing my basily fingers and feeling the encouraging drum of hope. And as silly as it sounds, there, in the vegetable aisle of the 24-hour Aldi, I felt predestined to be a cherished individual and that the world would wipe clean all of my hardships because I had immense, yet to be discovered, though feathered upon, value.

When I got home I had six messages on my phone. The green flashing felt like a warning and I knew something had happened. I thought Maniac had found out that Red loved me. It was becoming an impossible situation and I resented the drama. I wanted a quiet life to read and write and cook and bloom inside. I was sick of meth heads and depressive drunks and unpaid bills. I'd only just figured out that stillness was a form of active art and I wanted more of it. My past did not merge with my sauce dream. I put my groceries in the fridge and reluctantly pressed play. Five messages were from Red. Each message was increasingly persistent and spilled into the others. He was high. Crazy. On meth, on skunk, I couldn't tell. He was angry, so angry with me for withdrawing my love. "Let's tell them," he said, "let's tell everyone and move to the coast – back to California – you can, I don't know, watch the waves and write and shit and I can work construction – we can get a dog, a big slobbering idiot, fuck school, you've been to school, they can't teach you anything, don't you know that? Don't you know what you are to me? Why it hurts that you won't call me back? I'm telling you I'll walk that dog while you're writing your shit and we'll be happy and look back at this time and laugh because I will have given it all up for you because you will have given it all up for me because I want to be with you – but fuck it, okay, fuck it – you don't get it do you? This is who you fucking are and that will never change – ever – no matter what you do or where you go – you will never escape that. Call me back and I'll tell you about my buddy who has this dog who's about to have pups – I'm serious about California, I love you. Don't be so mean."

The sixth message was from Maniac. Red had shot himself in the head with a 12-gauge shot-gun. He died an hour after they reached the hospital. I could tell from her voice that she didn't know that Red and I were lovers. I dropped the phone and ran to the bus station. On the ride home, the sun rose and spilled across the fields and I thought of his beautiful head. I'd like to tell you that I cried (I did) and I wailed (I did) and that I beat myself up with guilt (I did, I did) but I only remember those moments like facts someone has told me. Mostly, I remember feeling the spread of something cold and numbing and eternal and how I knew for certian that it would never leave me, that I would never again be light, that I would have to consciously unpick my heart every time I wanted to unlock it, to use it or give it to somebody, I'd have to coax it from its hole and hold it in my hand like a newt or something as small and vulnerable. So in that way, Red was right, there would be no escaping who I was. The idea of this future seemed so historic and monumental, wet stone slab on the forehead monumental, when hours before, in another lifetime, the future had been bowls of white steaming at the table and laughter and windows. So while I mourned him, I also cried for her, the girl standing alone inside the florescence of 24-hour commerce, smelling tomatoes on the vine and thinking her life could be different, believing the path would be simple because she'd finally been chosen, chosen by herself, which is what youth is and why we miss it when it leaves us. I knew that the key to my unpicking would come in the shape of words, but they not would arrive through creaky floorboards and ancient mariner furniture, they would not shift like whispers through the fronds of my potted ferns, instead they'd take me skin snagging through a sharp, incurable blackness, like a skinned rabbit that is still alive will make a run for its pitiful life.

Asshole picked me up from the Greyhound station. Incredibly, he wanted a comfort shag, so I took him to the bar instead. We rang the others and he started buying everyone shots of vodka in Red's honor. Maniac suited her role as unmarried widow, sat in the booth smoking a joint and deciding which passage of Kahlil Gibran she was going to read at his funeral. They spoke of how distant he'd become. How his character had changed. Maniac said, "He went a bit psycho, you know, racing bikes, doing shit he shouldn't, but I wasn't his mom, right, I wasn't gonna tell him what to do with his life cuz he was always kinda like that, he was always a dare-devil, that's the life he wanted. Here, here!" Another shot and lemon. "You wouldn't have no-ticed," they told me, "because you were away at school, but he had started painting, though he sucked at it. I think it gave him peace, you know, so thank you," Maniac looked straight at me, "for being such an influence, there is no doubt he lived a full life," she said. We all agreed, yes, in the way that only eighteen-year-olds can feel complete.

I took the bus back to my apartment the day after the funeral and burnt each recipe, one by one, in the bathtub, then I went to bed for four months. After a year of anxiety fuelled self-destruction where I lost everything – my job, my scholarship, my dignity – I met a poet in a bar. I could tell he liked me, yet I couldn't face my value, so I repelled him by telling him that I'd loved someone who had shot himself. I said I'd found him, brain splattered against the wall. I told him I had cleaned it up and called the police. It was a lie and it wasn't a lie. I wanted to hear myself say it aloud, as punishment, for my mind played that scene over and over like a perverse penance. Those were the events my body was reacting to because I should have been there, you see, I should have been with him. So that was the situation I'd been reliving, smelling, choking on in the night, and we become our experiences, real or imaginary. Now, I know that the truth is always its most exposed inside a lie. That people use lies like spells to protect the terrible parts of their being, the parts that are so raw they remain defenceless, otherwise, otherwise, how could we live with all that we are? How could we desire, despite it all, our own realization?

Redneck

Humans and cultures respond
like rubber bands to change, they narrow and narrow,
becoming very thin until they snap under the applied pressure of
internal contradiction.

When I feel this tension, it means my unconsciousness is trying to part
an opening towards a reality,

which I can seldom explain beyond the sense that it had been
missing, and I had not known to look for it, and so, occurred in me
as a life I might have lived,

a dreamed life, a spirit limb life.
To examine it, is to actualize its flesh, its utility.
To ignore it, to leave it unanswered, is to wrap it in a story that
connects to all the other stories I've created for my delusions – the
subjects that remain
unfilled are the beginning of myths.

Myths behave in unreasonable ways
because they are works of fiction we base our truths upon.

It is hard to stop a fiction when it's trumpeted as a fact.
Freedom is fiction.

Though, we felt free. We felt in control
of our lives because we had been told
that we were, so kept looking beyond our dissatisfaction.
The best lies are also half-truths.

With such abstraction, how can you argue
anything but your own authority?

Reason is liberating in ways that myths are not
because it produces two forms of expansion.
The brain and the soul.
By soul, I mean an internal structure of emotional analysis

that can be built upon, until it learns to respond beyond
the reactionary, until the brain, strengthened through awareness, can
use it for climbing out of itself.

We are connected by our histories, yes, but, also, by our deviations
– the collective myths we've agreed upon. Those that justify our
contradictions and hush our fears of emptiness.

To understand the story of ourselves we need to admit and find a
way to empathize with our contradictions. Contradiction is found
in all our systems: religious, educational, economic, political. If
contradiction is unexamined it gravitates towards its cohort,

entitlement, and lays the foundation of fanaticism.
But it does not have to end this way.
Each life, each period of time, is orbital.

We can come back from our mistakes.

The thing to remember is,
regardless of your system of belief,

all delusions end
in hate.

How could they not?

The immoral impulse, like it's opposite, compassion, never dies.

Instead, it sleeps. A virus called repression. Hidden in the forgotten places.

Having sought the soiled breath of the
malnourished, spore-like it settles on the skin and digs
until scratching becomes a commonplace cut
that slowly bleeds the logic out.

A fear bruising ideas of disgust
that feel perfectly natural, spiritual even, and so, the host, the
disciple, must devise a myth to hold the hallucination in place.

The virus knows that facts cannot penetrate myths.

A myth takes the identity imagination gives it.

And, nothing has worked to shape our species more
than our ability to believe our own fabrications.

Except, perhaps, our longing
to understand why we need them.

It is from this longing, this desire to satisfy
the paradox we've created between fact and story,

that we find the power to deliberately
evolve or blind ourselves,

which could also be said
of love.

War

A country barbecue. Hank on. 4 x 4 double-cab Chevys or Dodges arriving on gravel. Only salads with mayo – potato, Waldorf, seven layer – corn on the cob, pie.

Venison, beef in all its forms, chicken, sausages cooking in their juices. J.D. and Coke and disposable cups for the keg of Bud. Coors in a can.

The smell of chewing tobacco spat on the grass, cigarettes, the evening's release of the cornfields heat. "You ain't a vegetarian now are ya?" "Not yet." And there's palpable relief.

Nobody stands too close to me, they watch me from over their cans and under their caps that read Carhartt or John Deer or Bass Pro, deciding if they recognize anything. It feels like an inquisition. I pretend to be admiring the yard art, an assortment of Fourth of July knickknacks.

Someone's kid pulls up on a four-wheeler. "Hey," I ask him, "can I please have go?" and he looks at his dad, who nods and says, "Keep your thumb on the trigger for her so's the motor stays running," which he politely does.

"Thanks," I say and take off. I ride off towards the mown and open fields, past creeks and cattle and corn. I haven't done this in years. I ride until there is nothing but sky and field and wind in the husks and me. Then, I turn around. When I got back they cheered and gave me a plate of food.

"We saved it for ya cuz some things never change, that sonnabitch over there he still eats all the damn sausages." The man they were talking about had just come back from his tour in Iraq. His mouth was full so he just waved his sausage. "Ready for your present," he said and patted me on the back.

"Don't look so nervous girl," he said, and turned to sausage man, "Hey, put your wiener down, you're scaring the ladies," and laughed. "Naw, we made ya somethin'. An invention." He went into the garage and returned with a leaf blower. Duct taped to the end of it was a thin cylinder and attached to that was an industrial-size roll of toilet paper. "Watch this," he said, and turned it on. The whole roll was airborne in twenty seconds. There were two of them, so we divided into teams and ran around the yard shooting one another with toilet paper for an hour.

"You gonna pick that up," shouts his wife, a toddler on her hip, "I don't even know why I bother with the yard," she tells a circle of friends."You love it," he smacks her softly on the bum as he runs by. "I won't be lovin' nothin' tonight if you don't keep your boots outta my hostas!" She hands her toddler to a friend and joins us.

We run and run until we can't stop laughing and have to sit down and drink beer. Between shots of Jagger, I catch up on the gossip. Who has died. Whose behavior should have killed them, but hasn't. Who's in Iraq, who's recently back, who leaves soon. Who has been injured. Who's married, divorced, or remarried, and all the stories why love went good or bad. The names of kids.

Later, with full stomachs and drunken intimacy, an old friend leans over and asks me, "What's it like living with them?"

"It's different," I say, thinking of London and my normal night of fun that includes satire and dinner parties, "I guess it's more reserved. I mean don't get me wrong, I love the Brits but ..." He cuts me off, "Nah, nah, I don't mean the Brits, we fight wars together 'n' shit, I'm talkin' about the Arabs. Ain't London full of 'em?"

Everybody stops to listen. It was so silent you could hear the breeze in the walnut trees, a commercial coming from the stereo in the garage, a dog barking. "Oh, well, actually, you know what, we have neighbors from Pakistan and they're really nice, you know, family people. I guess the truth is that I don't even think about it."

The walnut trees and the beginning cords of "All My Ex's Live in Texas." "Well, you jus' be careful, cuz that's how they get good people, by foolin' them inta thinking they're family people," he said. "No, they really are family people. I think they were all born in the UK," I said. "You're right, a few are homegrown and they use their families, boy, I seen it all the time on tour, and then one day, bam, you find out they've been plannin' shit and then everythin' jus' blows the fuck up."

I didn't know what to say to this. Many things flashed through my mind. I tried to remember when I last believed what I was told about the reasons for war. It was when his older brother and most of the boys in that graduating year were shipped to Afghanistan. I had wrapped a yellow ribbon, along with my entire community, around the oak tree outside our front door and felt that they were protecting our freedom. Although this man had served in Iraq and would probably serve again, he had only a war-torn experience of Muslims, whereas I encountered them in the everyday. "Honestly, I don't know your experience, but in mine, they're just normal people," he interrupted me. "It ain't normal to be so violent," he said.

Everybody here had a small arsenal at home and all the trucks parked in the driveway had loaded 12 gauges in their gun racks. It seemed to me that both groups of people lived in fear of the world they'd been left out of. How could I tell him that he was describing himself? I opened my mouth to speak and he punched me on the arm, "Relax girl, I didn't mean to get so serious on ya and all that," and he gave me a big hug. "Damn it's good to have you back. This is where you belong and we all love ya. Aw, don't you cry now, you gonna make me cry and I'm a six-foot-five big bubba who cries ugly."

I decide to leave. I need to be alone. I don't know if I've done anyone justice. I run over things I should have said in my head. Why did I cry? I feel like a fool. I feel helpless.

It's dusk and I take the back roads home to avoid the interstate. Fireflies in the ditches and the crickets whirr. Queen Anne's lace lit up like embroidery in my headlights and switch grass. My windows are down and I am alone on the road. The smell of hot gravel, mown hay, and the poignant vinegar of hogs. A whippoorwill and jackdaw, calling their names. Purple clouds trail through the last bit of sun like freight trains. To love this place is to contradict who I have become. It feels like a curse I'll never outlive, never lift.

When I was explaining evolution to my mother she said, "Stop it, I don't want to hear it, what I don't know won't kill me." That's wrong. What you don't know is always the thing that kills you. What you don't know is a hidden beast that you eat or you feed.

The Rapture of the Radicalized

Fascism happens when a society identifies more with myths,
than with reality. Evangelism breeds fascism because it perpetuates and
combines the fiction of spiritual entitlement and fantasy deliverance.

It is impossible to debate with people who expect the unraveling,
destruction of the earth, and, on some level, rejoice in it, because it
legitimizes their prophecy and brings them closer to their God.

Because of the population's readiness to believe in fantasy storylines
and Trump's preacher tactics, he has become a symbol religious
fanatics can relate to on a blind, yet devotional, level that feels linked
to their faith, which is also a parable presented as salvation.

The trouble with believing parables as reality is that you lose the
ability to reason, become accustomed to defending religious fantasies
over evidential science, until you actually begin to mistrust facts all
together and fall prey to extremism.

The irony is that a Trumpster extremist has more in common with a
Muslim extremist than they do with a white, wealthy politician, but
both are blind to this correlation because brainwashing relinquishes
the opportunity to acquire the knowledge necessary to think beyond
irrational and devotional patterns.

Fanaticism obliterates the idea that complex thought even exists as a separate system, because fanaticism damns all systems that ask questions. This has nothing to do with intelligence and everything to do with education and the gross discrepancy of opportunities in education is a human tragedy.

Thinking is a luxury. The luxury of thinking is a greater form of capital than any financial advancement.

When you are born middle or upper class you take thinking, like confidence, for granted. But complex thought is a muscle. How do you expect it to develop if you never actually use it because you are a fieldworker who is too exhausted, stressed, and worried about winter coats, food, shoes, dental insurance, and rent to be concerned about world affairs?

Poverty makes needs immediate, and basic survival keeps one basic. It keeps one from learning because it is impossible to see beyond the proximity of subsistence, plus there is not an equal educational system in place to show you how. In this scenario, rapture feels like justice, like getting what you deserve for the penance of your birthright. It gives the illusion that the hardship is worthwhile.

It is no coincidence that dictators the world over, without exception, have a history of culling education for their people and their laboring forces. Keeping one fixed in the myth means they are easy to manipulate. The first thing you learn when you begin to unlearn the myth is how to question. Can our leaders control us when we demand real, factual answers? No, not in a democracy, not yet, and we need to hang on to this by understanding that our very sense of humanity is at risk when corporations own the government.

It is better for corporate government to keep its laboring forces believing in their freedom and the afterlife then daring to demand rights as a human on this earth. It is better for corporate government to perpetuate and actually encourage the prejudices that ignorance and fanatical religion systematically encourages so that all the laboring people – fieldworkers, be they Asian, indentured white, redneck, Middle Eastern, Indian, African, Aboriginal, Hispanic and so on – fight among themselves and blame one another without ever realizing the truth of their power, which is, divided they remain minority groups, united they become a force that can overthrow.

Rapture, in an allegorical sense, represents a hive mind that desires, above all else, revolution. Imagine if that power was emancipated through education. It would change everything.

Instead they enslave you to identity propaganda by making you believe that the undereducated, working-class, under-class, God-fearing, white fieldworkers of the USA are salt-of-the-earth simple men and women wanting to live simple lives.

There is nothing wrong with living a simple life and that is a noble ambition. But this group identity is manipulated by corporate and political myths that discredit, destroy, and mute your voices so they can prostitute you for your labors, be those farming, factory, voting, military, or any of the industrial cogs that machines will eventually replace.

What will become of you then? With your body full of cancers, and your hands of little use? Keeping you a mind-numbed machine means that they don't have to recognize you as human.

Uniting in propaganda, only seeking half-truths, robs you of your voice as a respected human being. It robs you of your rights to a fair working wage. It robs you of your rights to clean drinking water, clean soil. It robs you of your rights to health care and job prospects. It keeps you in your place, your class. But, mostly, it robs you of your rights to respectability and accountability within our global community by keeping you purposely misinformed and isolated.

Which means that the rest of the world feels as though it's closing in on you and foreign in skin, religion, and mindset. I am not saying that you must agree with opposing opinion, but that all opinions deserve your full investigation, prior to your trust.

Because when people don't understand something they become fearful, and when they are fearful they become angry, and when they are angry they learn to hate. Hate is easier than assimilation, for the person and all of their governing agencies. Hate is easier to control than love. So uniting in a shared myth of misrepresentation is robbing yourself of your human capacity for love.

And we can only love to the level of consciousness we've reached. Which is why the love and compassion fanaticized Evangelists share and show the world is disproportionate to the love and compassion they profess to have as a Christians.

It is this hypocrisy, not their faith, which turns them into extremists, for hypocrisy is the cornerstone of radicalism. And the more disconnected, insignificant, and snubbed they feel, the more defensive they become, until they are, preposterously, defending their right to remain uninformed .

Which turns a lack of education into a use value, a labor power ripe for exploitation, abuse, and the devastation of our glorious planet.

Ecology

When I was young, we swam in the lake every summer. It was our holiday. Snapping turtles would bite our toes and swim, with their little thumb heads, next to us. We would fish, catch frogs, and float around on big inner tubes drinking pop. By the end of summer our swimsuits were a murky brown, as was our skin. Silt would collect in my hair so that each curl could crunch and turn to dust in my palm. We kept our fish in a bucket until it was time for filleting, then we'd fry them up with salt, pepper, flour, and eggs, while the adults sat on lawn chairs drinking beer and giving instructions. After we ate, we'd play hide-and-seek in the twilight, wrestle, catch fireflies, and, at last, fall in a tired circle and talk until we fell asleep in a bundle like bear cubs. Listening to the loons and the bang of a screen door and the fuse of a lighter, that crisp burn and someone's laughter. By the time we were carried up to bed, the world had gone silent.

Sometimes, now, when my children come in from playing in the woodland, they carry the smell of the lake in the sweat at the napes of their necks. I inhale them for as long as they'll let me, freezing inside the shrill ache of love, this moment that I know I'll think of as proof of a life well lived when it comes my time to die.

I took my children to the lake last summer. I told them all the stories and wanted them to have adventures too. We brought fishing poles, a Styrofoam cup of earthworms, and inner tubes. I cleaned out a mayonnaise jar, peeled off its label, and punched holes in the lid so that the fireflies could breath in their new home.

When we got to the lake we found an algae as florescent as Ghostbusters slime was scummed across its surface. "What on earth is that?" I asked, and pulled my children away from the water.

"It won't hurt them none, it just looks bad, but we've all been swimming in it, even the babies, and we're fine. Just fine." He dipped his foot in to show me it didn't hurt.

I started taking out sandwiches so I could feed my children, and then make them wait for an hour before swimming. I needed time to come up with excuses to keep them from the water, because the only other option would be incriminatory and disrespectful of everyone else's decisions.

"What caused it?" I asked and tried to sound casual, I could feel, already that they thought I was overreacting, but I was horrified.

"Don't know, could be the farm run off, but I've been taking the boat out every night and dropping in crystals," he wiped the green slime from his foot and onto a towel."What kind of crystals?"

"Just some shit I got online that's meant to burn off the algae and it works sometimes too, for a bit anyway, but I'll tell you what, it's great for fishing! Suckers just come straight to the surface. Dead on arrival fish fry. Don't even know what hit 'em."

Mirrors

I live in an extremely liberal city. I wouldn't have it any other way.
It's where I feel comfortable. It is the opposite to where I've lived as a
child, and having the experience of both places has taught me things
of value. To title yourself as Liberal (which I do by default) seldom
means you are without prejudice. It often means that you have simply
chosen a prejudice that is tolerable within your societal group, which,
incidentally, is the same model for groups of bigotry everywhere,
because prejudice only works when it's bred with self-righteousness. It
is entirely acceptable to be prejudiced against rural America in liberal
company. It would be utterly intolerable if the derogatory comments
that I hear, often and continuously, about rural Americans were
said about any other societal, racial, or religious group. I notice that
projecting a self-righteousness into the world is to ally yourself with
groups that you profess to despise. Because it's our polarized views that
keep us locked in circles, where feelings of superiority form a sense of
entitlement that carries the same response of division.

Instead of asking who is responsible, we need to ask, how am I
responsible?

Otherwise, we risk becoming mirrors of one another who hate what
we see without realizing it is a version of ourselves, broadcast from
the same sanctimonious claims.

I believe that leveling with the notion of superiority, as groups of humans or humans over other living things, would create an incomprehensible wave of compassion, unequal to any other act of peace humanity has ever performed.

True anarchy is finding connectivity within the ideas we despise and linking threads of conversation without judgment. A judgment is a judgment still and best only made of our own actions, for those are the only ones we can profess to understand.

True anarchy is not a moral standing, rather a rising to the challenge of finding a pathway of tolerance, despite conditioning circumstance.

I fear the current reality is a world that's producing fewer critical and compassionate thinkers because it is stuck in the rhetoric of extremism and capitalism, which rely on the proliferation of mass oblivion.

Rural Americans are a minority group with a gamut of social problems like other minority groups and they need to be accepted and supported by the nation if we ever want to truly combat racism. They suffer record levels of drug abuse, grinding poverty, at-risk religious fanaticism, substandard education, and isolation. Inside these fringe communities parables flourish to make the adversity endurable.

The lack of critical thinking skills combined with unchallenged, exploitative dogma and the normalization of hateful narrative create the groundwork for a radicalization that moves terrifying ideologies into hyper speed.

We need to recover the language of compassion, which has enabled us, in the past, to overthrow dictatorships, regenerate impoverished areas with hospitals, schools and jobs, and de-radicalize an indoctrinated populace. This is exactly what our country is crying out for, it is exactly the type of social democracy our fieldworkers and laborers are pleading to have. But because we are stuck in old identities of predestination, individualism, and superiority, we cannot see how our country is under threat from a breed of terrorism that we have each had a role in producing.

As an America living in England, I am constantly asked, "How can your people believe in Trump?" Most of these people have never met a rurally raised American. Most of these people are the beneficiaries of the Land of the Free and capitalism where the clean world is experienced and networked. Trump happens when both sides of the populace make decisions based around manufactured ideas that protect them from the others' reality.

It is not unchristian to demand that our spiritual and governmental leaders uphold a transparent moral civility. Christianity arose from those that were brave enough to question heretics. The questioning and challenging of a tyrannical heresy is the very foundation of Christianity. It is, however, entirely unchristian to knowingly pardon the cruel maltreatment of another human.

There is no simple reason why a person joins a hate group. However, research shows that the reason variables fall under associated feelings of alienation, hopelessness, and humiliation derived from a lack of social and economic opportunities.

Crucial to successful prevention and reintegration from radicalization include listening and working within communities at a local level, establishing trust and public-driven leadership, and openly identifying recruiters and financiers of terrorism.

Call out the heretics. Refuse to purchase from exploitative corporations. Organize citizens' assemblies. Understand that it is arrogant to believe that terrorism happens in corners of the world independent of your actions. Evolve our national identity by utilizing the collective power of a counter-narrative that truly represents this land and all of her peoples.

Redneck

We are all the by-products of our collective myths.

Nothing, no thing, or institution exists
that hasn't first been seeded inside of human imagination.

The myths we've created work to control us.
Even the myth of our own autonomy

means we only unite when forced
by extremities of injustice.

The fact that we can imagine it otherwise
means it can be otherwise, should we choose,

cohesively, to let go of the old narratives
that no longer serve what our species has become.

There is power in the knowledge that our levels of violence
are matched by our levels of empathy.

This is because when one force rises, so does its opposite.
If we could focus our collective intentions

we could move ourselves from the era of shadow
and into the era of informed and universal contemplation.

In my early memories I am often drawing boats –
Nina, Pinta, Santa Maria – transformed by my imagination and box
of crayons. I was land locked; there were waves in the grasses, the
dust, the clouds, but no wild ocean.

For me, the ocean was mysterious, as was the cosmos, and being a
religious child, mysterious notions were rinsed, like the head of babes,
in salvation. I learnt how to tell stories about things I'd never seen.

I folded my drawings into small, palm-sized squares
and stuck them inside my pillowcase. In the abyss of night,
I would rub the cloth over the squares of my fleet,
position them in an arrow and imagine myself as a living figurehead.

Hair tangled, the spray of salt, the escape of fate, and into civilization,
which I expected to behave as a chart of experience that unfolded with
each realm of possibility. In my head, my measure of civilization grew,
similar to the celestial sky that grows into its changing self as the boat
traverses. Distance seemed implicit, as did the pushing forward.
The ship pressing and moving through a force of untold depth.
All the necessary components of mythmaking.

We analyze a myth after it's been fixed into our narration
and it feels like a prophecy.

When I met my husband, twenty years later, we walked to the river
of our university town and spoke of boats and fell in love. Love
happens inside the mysteries you discover you've shared.

The secret of love is sharing a secret. Just like
the secret of manipulation is holding a secret ransom.

You don't realize your strength, I tell my mother, but those that hurt you
know it well. Create a pathway for your power.

We create things.
All aspects of civilization extend
from this defining moment in our animals' history.

To create is what humans do, what we've always done,
and around the things we've created we build our stories
so that the two are inseparable, interlaced hands.
It is important to actively create because
once released, our creation survives inside a story
that context turns into a fluid creature.

In our culture's current fluidity of truth, the story of dogma
has become the story of our expiration.
But we recreate our truths by changing the context of our storylines
into tales that we can love. Which makes sense because

the greatest unknown in anything is its capacity to love.
And, to hate is to irrationally fear the loss of something you love,
which could be a person, an idea, or your understanding of your
place in the world.

To love something is to make it erasable and our utmost fear is erasure.
Humans do not want to feel erasure.

So, held ransom to our fear of obliteration, we create the conditions
that guarantee erasure by insisting that inequality is a personal
freedom, the mask for tyranny.

Our idea of freedom is also a fluid creature composed of language
and mirage and the rhythms that magnetize our preverbal devotions.

Where we translate our stories into the truths we want to maintain
rather than the truths that present themselves as real.

Story can behave groundlessly –
it can make monsters from nothing,

saints from nothing if its translators use words
that embody emotions that trigger
the instinctive trappings of the current time.

What we say now we say for history.
Shorn of our choices and wavering between defining moments.

Denuding. Many of us, sheep to an algorithm that behaves like
an organism directing its host. You. Me. We host our culture. The
bacteria of our choices, our creations, eat from us.

Why not? It has always been the case that every body on this earth
requires a sensitive balance of organisms.

All bodies on this earth, human, water, narrative, soil are experiencing
a form of physical and or emotional chaos, and small changes, over
time, can reprogram an entire system.
Infection works the same way. Spittle. A cough. A word.
We can infect our culture though discourse.

The outliers of any current culture, from petri dish to economies,
create their own bacteria. And that is where we have found our cures.
Here, in the translation of disease.

Here, where the pathway from experience to meaning to application
is so personal and subjective that speaking the same language
is secondary to what is being (or not being) understood.

We need to feel our words again. We need to access that
chamber locked in the preverbal universe
where words are musical performances.

And language is
a known creature.

Individuals Do Not Exist

We are told, or rather, sold, as a group, the idea that individuality represents personal freedom, but nothing could be further from the truth. We are measured as consumers, legions of workers, voters, viewers, likes, units. As long as we profess our imaginary independence from the group, we are powerless and neutered against human injustice. A group mentality is the most powerful force in humanity. Thinking of ourselves, our actions, as a part of a united human muscle, a collective identity, is to belong to one another, to our earth, in a way that recovers our lost human value.

We need to rise above the ideology of sole individualism. It's just an idea, after all, adopted as a fact during our present time, but different times necessitate different ideas and as we are entering a new phase of humanity, it feels suicidal to give our greatest powers over to corporations who control our sense of humanity by enchanting us into false values for their profit. The mysteries we seek are within intentional collective thought. We have two compulsions as humans. The compulsion to create and the compulsion to destruct. Collective living, as a member of the planet, life beyond the individual, yet a part of a bigger collection of thought, cures incalculable loneliness that's plagued our peoples and keeps one living as a creator, not a destructor.

Also, we are too populated to achieve equality through individuality; our resources, our opportunities are unevenly distributed for any one person to live or adopt a mindset of individuality and profess to believe in humankind. Incidentally, economic intelligence gathers its information from our human hive, the Internet, where we are placed inside of collective patterns and directed. A chosen collective identity is an antidote, a counterbalance that contradicts patterns controlled by the few and allows us to regain our strength as a species.

The flux is not the problem. Our cultures have always been in flux. We are quickly reaching the point where we can no longer expand on this planet. Surely the next stage for us would be an expansion of the mind. Our minds being the least collectively explored part of our earth. Surely the conscience shift from individuality to group contemplation is one of the next stages of evolution. The idea of individualized self-expression must end. The idea of individuality must end, not least because it is psychologically limiting, but also because it is a great enabler of seclusion, environmental extermination, and social divide.

A shift in popular patterns is one of the social mainstays of adaptation. It happens in every era. Take when women were denied the right to vote, for instance, or slave ownership. These obscene constructs were the norm. Now, their practice is marginalized and although we are still feeling the fractured repercussions of these circumstances, we culturally recognize them as invalid and unethical ideas. Now, it is time to move beyond mere developments of physical progress, however important they continue to be, and focus on expanding our cerebral frontiers. Because giving women the right to vote and abolishing slavery did not cure misogyny or racism, only intellectual unity can do that, which is an example of why ideas are worth fighting for.

We have witnessed the power of group mentality on countless occasions, but the implication has always been that one must be physically present to be effective or powerful. Change is not a physical infection. We can adopt different ideas. We can imagine ourselves collectively.

We dynamically use language to define or redefine our relationships with the living, with objects, and memory. Language has to be actively guarded from obscuring the truth because, now more than ever, words are circumstantial and shifting in meaning. Think of how the words progress, individualism, expression, freedom can change when used as propaganda. When you build empires on fluctuating meanings, you end up with unrealistic definitions of place and self.

The contradictions between liberty and equality have existed and remain until we fracture from the systems that work to divide or classify us and join or at least recognize collective thought as a commonality that we are engaging with or without our knowledge.

It is not possible to live a life without contradiction and I am not suggesting that we eradicate it, in fact creative and cultural growth demand its existence. To clash is not to fail. To clash is to admit the need for a new type of culture.

When I think of a new culture I see the end of us, extinction, death at the moment when we are only just beginning to understand all that it means to be living. Annihilation by delusion. But. I also see compassion, communication, creation thriving as a living organism that lattices our species and becomes its own algorithm where our minds work as a typographical storyboard, where creativity and critical analysis become social colonies of expression, working towards the goal of global narration.

We begin by thinking it so.

Redneck

The night holds us differently to the day.
The night becomes a pursued ingestion that halts with first light.
The day is for dissolving what has been absorbed,
knowing it there. Feeling it there. Moon in a sunlit sky.

I walk the abandoned train tracks to the place we called "the trestle."

Drainage ditches of the mind and Black-eyed Susan's floating.
Under the sky, I am free to press against the window of myself,
to shell scrumped walnuts, watch birds, and make worlds of my own.

Later, at the kitchen sink, scrubbing my stained fingers with Dial and
a brush. I think of how I know a different language in this country,
one I had tried to forget, shun even, but that was the wrong response.

That was the response that ends in Nowhere, speaks of Nobody.

I want to remember it all now. To give it a purpose, and with that
purpose, a new life, that writing fixes into the larger memory of
humanity that art is collating. That is, the memory of how humans
survived. Which is to say, how much they loved. Or didn't.

My mother is asleep on the sofa.
She has been discharged after months of hospitalization, and
although she needs constant care and is a long way from walking,
she's alive.

I chop carrots in the kitchen and a little warbler lands on the
birdfeeder, pecks at the seeds I've just replenished, and flies away. The
Neighbour walks across the yard with a Get-Well card. I smile at her
through the window and meet her at the backdoor. She says her son
will mow my mother's yard.

Suddenly I feel an immense sense of hope.

All around us, right now, there are small signs of encouragement,
creating hands that can reach into the tornados of ourselves
and grab hold of solid and convincing clues –

which are often small kindnesses encircling average lives. Slip notes
inside a universal wind that speak of who we are, who we might dare
to become, because the greatest changes are based around decisions
made in the face of what feels like madness, think of evolution, think
of disease,

think of what a cell can do.

NO PARKING
DOLLAR
GENERA
GUN SHOW
FRI SAT SUN
FAIRGROUNDS
ADEL

128

JONES FAMILY

Spike's

Spike's Barber
Shop
will be
CLOSED
until further
notice.

Thank you.

www.ingramcontent.com/pod-product-compliance
Lightning Source LLC
Chambersburg PA
CBHW021843090426
42811CB00033B/2120/J